IRELAND'S DISEASE

IRELAND'S DISEASE
The English in Ireland
1887

Paschal Grousset

with an Introduction by
Constance Ramillon Conner
1986

THE
BLACKSTAFF
PRESS
BELFAST AND WOLFEBORO, NEW HAMPSHIRE

*First published in 1887
by George Routledge and Sons
This Blackstaff Press edition is a photolithographic
facsimile of the George Routledge and Sons edition of 1888,
printed by Bradbury, Agnew & Company*

*This edition published in 1986
by The Blackstaff Press
3 Galway Park, Dundonald, Belfast BT16 OAN, Northern Ireland
and
27 South Main Street, Wolfeboro, New Hampshire 03894 USA*

© *Introduction, Constance Ramillon Conner, 1986
All rights reserved*

*Printed in Northern Ireland
by
The Universities Press Limited*

*British Library Cataloguing in Publication Data
Grousset, Paschal
Ireland's disease: the English in
Ireland, 1887. — New ed.
1. Ireland — Social conditions
1. Title
941.5081   HN400.3.A8*

*Library of Congress Cataloging-in-Publication Data
Grousset, Paschal, 1844–1909.
Ireland's disease.
Reprint. Originally published: London; New York:
G. Routledge, 1888.
Includes index.
1. Ireland—Description and travel—1801–1900
2. Ireland—Social Life and customs—19th century.
3. Ireland—Social conditions. 1. Title.
DA975.G89   1986   941.5081   86-17545*

ISBN 0 85640 370 9

INTRODUCTION TO THE 1986 EDITION

No less an authority than Gladstone hailed *Ireland's Disease* as 'the most weighty and important inquiry and judgement upon the history and state of Ireland published by any foreigner for half a century'. The approbation of the 'grand old man' was expressed in a letter sent from his home, Hawarden, to George Routledge and Sons, the publishers, when the book came out in London early in December 1887. The *Pall Mall Gazette* of December 9 quoted what it described as Gladstone's 'flaming certificate as to the excellence of *Ireland's Disease*', and pointed out that the work had also been 'extolled' by *The Times*. The *Gazette* went on to underline this exceptional concordance of opinion between the great Liberal leader and the famous Conservative daily: 'A book on Ireland which elicits such superlative praise from Mr Gladstone and *The Times* has achieved a unique and almost impossible success.'

The French version, entitled *Les Anglais en Irelande* and, like the English edition, written under the pseudonym of Philippe Daryl, was brought out in January 1888 by the well known Parisian firm Hetzel & Company, Grousset's French publishers. Meanwhile, on December 30 1887, newspapers on both sides of the Channel acclaimed the fact that its author had been received by Gladstone in the vast suite overlooking the Place Vendôme where the ex-premier and his family were staying during a twenty-four-hour visit to Paris, *en route* for a holiday in Italy. Grousset was greeted with the utmost cordiality, and was presented to Gladstone's daughter. The visit lasted over an hour, and among various subjects British politics were discussed, including the Irish question.

After this flying start, *Ireland's Disease* received excellent reviews in all sections of the British press. In Ireland the *Freeman's Journal* was approving; but the *Nation* objected to Daryl's criticisms of the Catholic clergy.

The book originated in two series of articles on Ireland published in *Le Temps* during the summer of 1886 and the autumn of 1887. Paschal Grousset, writing as Philippe Daryl, had been a regular correspondent of this prestigious Parisian daily since 1877, and many of his articles and reviews were edited in book form in both England and France. The volume entitled *À Londres* is of special interest since it covers the political scene during the months of the third Gladstone ministry (January to June 1886) when Home Rule was the question of the day. Grousset interviewed Parnell's up-and-coming young lieutenants, Liberals who supported Gladstone, and the agricultural labourer and radical MP Joseph Arch. *À Londres* contains an appreciative article on John Morley, the newly-appointed Secretary for Ireland, and an analysis of Robert Giffen's proposals for Irish land reform.

From these articles Grousset emerges as a fervent admirer of Gladstone's electoral reforms of 1884, and of his championship of Irish autonomy. When, after the defeat of his first Home Rule Bill, Gladstone went to the country on the issue of Home Rule, *Le Temps* sent Grousset to Ireland as its special correspondent during the electoral campaign of June and July 1886. Fascinated by what he referred to as the 'sister isle', he returned for a longer period during the summer of 1887, when Balfour's policy of coercion with all that it entailed – suspension of the Habeas Corpus Act, special powers of search and of arrest on suspicion, the transfer of extra regiments to Ireland – was in full swing. The result of these visits was *Ireland's Disease*. Of its seventeen chapters, only chapter fifteen, half of sixteen – 'Scottish Ireland' – and seventeen did not appear in *Le Temps*.

Like most travellers of his time, Grousset first set foot in Ireland at Kingstown (now Dun Laoghaire) and took Dublin as his starting point. Quick to sense the difference in manners and appearance between English and Irish, he saw Dublin as 'the focus of a nationality', and noted the desire for Home Rule manifest in the city's statues, its flags, even in the goods displayed in its shops. He describes not only the public buildings and fashionable squares of Dublin, but also the poorer quarters, and he was horrified by the appalling poverty of the Liberties. Like Thackeray, whom he quotes, he observes that the slum-dwellers of Dublin 'love each other and know how to put their love into words'.

Once out of Dublin, he was enchanted by the Irish countryside; his description of the moist climate is reminiscent of Yeats's 'wet winds blowing/out of the clinging air'. We should recall that at the date of Grousset's visits to Ireland, Yeats was a young man beginning to publish his first poems; O'Casey and Joyce were small boys drinking in the atmosphere of the Dublin Grousset observed and appreciated; Somerville and Ross were starting their celebrated literary partnership, while George Moore was winning fame with his novels. The Ireland Grousset visited is present in all their works.

Grousset had an excellent knowledge of English, and he enjoyed the company of Irish people and the welcome held out to the 'Frenchie': he records that the 'Marseillaise' was whistled. . . 'saying plainly: – "You are French, and I am a friend of France, like all Irishmen."' Grousset mentions the numerous letters of introduction supplied to him by friends in London which opened doors to him in all classes of the population: he visited a doctor, a lawyer, a Belfast merchant, a land agent, etc. But above all, his contacts with the farming population in the various counties he passed through and with the emigrants waiting to leave for the New World at Queenstown (today Cobh) impressed upon him the economic situation of rural Ireland – the lack of investment in the land, the slump in agricultural prices, the rise of the ubiquitous moneylenders. He analyses the budget of an average, hardworking tenant of a twelve-acre farm, and describes the situation of seventeen smallholders whom he visited. From this inquiry emerges a picture of poverty and degradation, of tenants struggling under the weight of hopeless arrears of rent, and often facing eviction. Only among the Irish-speaking fishermen of Valentia Island did Grousset find the 'happy courage' of people who were free of rents and landlords.

Before setting foot in Ireland, Grousset had done his homework well by following the Irish question in the British press and by studying the Parliamentary papers of the time. He backs up his observations with official figures as he travels through Kerry on horseback, through Clare, Galway and Sligo by train, steamer and horse-and-trap. His approach to the regions visited, like that of another famous traveller, Robert Lloyd Praeger, is based on their geomorphology, and in the French version of his book he gives as his source the great French geographer Elie Reclus, whom he may well have known personally. Grousset is steeped in Irish legends and history, though understandably limited by the contemporary nationalistic and idealised view of early Ireland as a Celtic paradise. Once his historical synopsis reaches the eighteenth century he is on firmer ground: his admiration for Jonathan Swift impels him to quote extensively from *A Modest Proposal*. Arthur Young and Gustave de Beaumont hold a place of honour in his references, and when he recommends Irish novelists of the nineteenth century, the list is exhaustive.

A man of his time, Grousset believed in material progress. He hails with delight the excellent roads and railways which will, he considers, bring tourists from France and England to enjoy the wonderful scenery; he rejoices in the evident prosperity of the manufacturing centres of Belfast, Derry and Dundalk. What is more unusual, he foresees the importance trans-Atlantic communications will assume with the laying of the cables from Valentia, and he advocates the development of steamboat lines to America from the superb natural base of the Shannon estuary. A free-thinker and a Mason, he criticises the easy-living clergy, 'whose sleekness forms a striking contrast with the general emaciation of their parishioners'; but he has only words of respect for the touching sincerity of the faith of the Irish Catholic population. He realises the unique place held by the Catholic Church in the history of Ireland, thanks to the role played by its clergy in what Grousset names as 'resistance to the oppressor'. We know from his conversations at Westminster with certain young Parnellite MPs that he questioned the wisdom of the close alliance of the Irish Party and the Catholic Church; but where the National League (successor to the Land League) is concerned, he pays tribute to the importance of the work of priests. In this context, while Grousset admires the League's efficient organisation and favours the Plan of Campaign put into action from the autumn of 1886, he has reservations concerning the violence of the 'Moonlighters' and the justice of certain boycotts.

With hindsight, students of the 'Ulster question' will notice that Grousset compares favourably with the political leaders of the time – Gladstone, even Parnell – in that he took the Orangemen of the north seriously, and foresaw a possible army mutiny if the military were called upon to coerce the loyalists. Though he started out from London a convinced Home Ruler, his visits to 'Scottish Ireland', as he called it, brought home to him the extent of Unionist opposition a few months after the decision of Randolph Churchill to 'play the Orange card'. Grousset saw that the economic prosperity of north-east Ireland was linked to that of Great Britain. His proposals for the political statute of Ireland in the last chapter of *Ireland's Disease* include guarantees for the Protestant majority in Ulster, four provincial assemblies, and, in the last resort, a hegemony of the north-eastern counties with Scotland when Home Rule was granted to the rest of Ireland. For readers today, some of these suggestions are very close to ideas contained in the *New Ireland Forum Report* almost a hundred years later.

Grousset's proposals for land reform show similar originality. He foresees that the giving outright of small farms to the peasants would neither make for progress in agriculture nor insure against the rise of a new class of big landowners. His suggestions include the supervision of agricultural methods by a national trust body, the creation of a land bank, and the institution of model farms on the great estates. Run co-operatively, these last would serve as pioneer centres of experiment and training. He advised that the extent of all private farms should be limited to 500 acres – the *'Lex Licinia'* of ancient Rome. All this, obviously, implied the redistribution of land after the buying-out of the landlords, in accordance with the hopes of the agricultural labourers and small farmers – the left wing of the National League. Here, as in his conception of the British radicals as the natural allies of Ireland, Grousset's ideas coincide with those of his Irish contemporary Michael Davitt, whom he later came to know and admire. Grousset's solutions to the land question heralded those of such reformers as Horace Plunkett, George Russell and Dr Joseph Johnston.

Who, then, was this Frenchman who seems to have understood Ireland and her problems so well? He came to the forefront of French politics during the fateful year of 1870 which saw the outbreak of the Franco-Prussian war, the downfall of the emperor Louis Napoleon, and the siege of Paris. In March 1871 Grousset was elected to the Paris Commune. No study has hitherto been made of his life and work, perhaps because, though he was a socialist, he lies outside the main left-wing coteries of nineteenth-century France. Born in Corsica, brought up in the Tarn-et-Garonne, he came to Paris as a scholarship *lycéen* with a brilliant career in front of him. When studying medicine, he grew interested in republican politics, and took up journalism; he became the right-hand man of the famous pamphleteer Henri Rochefort, on the editorial staff of his widely read daily *La Marseillaise*. The well known series of articles in its columns by Karl Marx's eldest daughter, Jenny, on the ill-treatment of Fenian prisoners in English jails was probably Grousset's first introduction to the Irish question.

In January 1870 Grousset was the innocent cause of the assassination of a young colleague, Victor Noir, by the prince Pierre Bonaparte, the French emperor's cousin. The prince had attacked Grousset in an insulting article on Corsica; Grousset challenged him to a duel and sent his seconds, Victor Noir and another journalist, to arrange the place and the weapons. Pierre Bonaparte, probably mistaking Victor Noir for the celebrated journalist Rochefort, shot him out of hand. Noir's funeral was the signal for a huge anti-imperialist demonstration in Paris; ironically, Grousset was imprisoned for several months for having denounced the assassin in a series of articles! Released finally in July 1870, he volunteered as a soldier, took part in the defence of Paris against the Prussians, and was active in the *clubs des quartiers* which have been called the 'nurseries of workers' control'. And the workers did, in fact, finally take control. The antagonism between Paris, which had suffered great hardships during the siege, and the ultra-conservative government at Versailles, which had obliged the city to surrender and had made peace with the Prussians, came to a head on 18 March 1871. The Versailles authorities sent troops to commandeer the cannon which the people of Paris had subscribed for, but the National Guard – the citizens' army – resisted successfully. The next day the leaders of the National Guard called for elections to a Communal Council of the capital, the Commune, which would govern Paris as in the years 1789–95. Grousset was elected to it by the 18th *arrondissement,* and was appointed to the important post of delegate for external relations. His newspapers, published under the Commune, set out his belief in parliamentary democracy, free elections and universal suffrage. After the *Semaine Sanglante* during which 30,000 Communards were executed by the Versailles government's troops, he was captured and sentenced to penal servitude for life in the Île Ducos (New Caledonia). He lived there with Rochefort, François Jourde and Olivier Pain – all former journalists of *La Marseillaise* – from 1872 to 1874, when the four companions made history by carrying out the only successful escape by any of the thousands of Communards deported to the detested convict settlements. The news of this feat was met at first with total incredulity in French government circles.

Following a triumphant welcome in Australia, the four friends made their way to San Francisco, then to New York, and were fêted in both cities by Irish and French exiles. They decided to return to Europe; and once in England, Grousset and Jourde exposed in *The Times* the appalling conditions of the Communards in the penal settlements of New Caledonia. Like so many French exiles, Grousset chose to settle in London, where his cousin, Adrian Hébrard, administrator of *Le Temps,* eventually found work for him as a part-time correspondent for the newspaper. Grousset used several pseudonyms when writing for French newspapers during his exile, including those of Philippe Daryl and André Laurie. Among the French refugees in London, his closest friend seems to have been Jules Vallès, the famous left-wing novelist and essayist.

After the amnesty of 1880 Grousset lived partly in Paris, partly in London, contributing articles to *Le Temps* and several other papers, until his election to the National Assembly in 1893, when he came to live more permanently in Paris as deputy of Picpus, in the 12th *arrondissement*. He was regularly re-elected to this seat as an Independent Socialist. He defended Dreyfus in the famous controversy that shook the French establishment at the turn of the century, publishing pamphlets and articles in his favour, and he was also active in support of the trade-union movement.

In 1877, during the years of exile in London, Grousset –

or rather 'André Laurie' – became the collaborator of the celebrated novelist Jules Verne. Their partnership, thought up by the publisher Hetzel, was to last for well over twenty years. Much light has been thrown on this collaboration by Marc Soriano in his biography of Jules Verne. He attributes to Grousset the fact that *Les Cinq Cents Millions de la Bégum* is 'one of those rare novels of opinion of the second half of the 19th century that has remained powerful and up-to-date'. Writing of *P'tit Bonhomme,* a novel with an entirely Irish background, Soriano points out that 'for the first time, the Irish nationalist cause is analysed clearly, not only on the political but also on the economic and social plane', and it is likely that Grousset's influence on Verne can also be traced here. The link between the two men remained strong until Verne's death in 1905, when Grousset pronounced his funeral oration.

Grousset himself was to live four years longer; he died in Paris in the spring of 1909 and was buried in the cemetery of Père Lachaise, with a republican funeral – the tricolour flag draping the coffin, the bugles sounding. The newspapers of the day, *Le Temps, Le Figaro,* and Jaurès's paper, *L'Humanité,* recalled his life as a patriot and his services to France. Today, his name figures in history books as a member of the Commune and as a socialist deputy of the Third Republic; but nowhere has his work on Ireland been treated with the appreciation it deserves. The publication of this facsimile will, we hope, help to fill the gap.

Constance Ramillon Conner
1986

IRELAND'S DISEASE

NOTES AND IMPRESSIONS

BY

PHILIPPE DARYL

THE AUTHOR'S ENGLISH VERSION

LONDON
GEORGE ROUTLEDGE AND SONS
BROADWAY, LUDGATE HILL
GLASGOW AND NEW YORK
1888

LONDON
BRADBURY, AGNEW, & CO., PRINTERS, WHITEFRIARS.

PREFACE.

—◆—

THESE pages were first published in the shape of letters addressed from Ireland to *Le Temps*, during the summer months of 1886 and 1887.

A few extracts from those letters having found their way to the columns of the leading British papers, they became the occasion of somewhat premature, and, it seemed to the author, somewhat unfair conclusions, as to their general purport and bearing.

A fiery correspondent of a London evening paper, in particular, who boldly signed "J. J. M." for his name, went so far as to denounce the author as "an ally of the *Times*, in the congenial task of vilifying the Irish

Preface.

people by grotesque and ridiculous caricatures," which charge was then summarily met as follows :—

To the Editor of the PALL MALL GAZETTE.

SIR,—

Let me hope, for the sake of "J. J. M.'s" mental condition, that he never set eyes upon my Irish sketches in *Le Temps*, about which he volunteers an opinion. If, however, he has actually seen my prose in the flesh, and he still clings to his hobby that I am hostile to the Irish cause or unsympathetic with the Irish race, why then I can only urge upon his friends the advisability of a strait waistcoat, a brace of mad doctors, and an early berth in a lunatic asylum. I never heard in my life of a sadder case of raving delusion.

Yours obediently,

PHILIPPE DARYL.

PARIS, *September* 18, 1887.

Thus ended the controversy. There was no reply.

Allowance should be made, of course, for the natural sensitiveness of Irishmen on everything that relates to their noble and unhappy country. But, what! Do they entertain, for one moment, the idea that everything is right and normal in

Preface.

it? In that case there can be no cause of complaint for them, and things ought to remain as they are. All right-minded people will understand, on the contrary, that the redress of Irish wrongs can only come out of a sincere and assiduous exposure of the real state of affairs, which is not healthy but pathological, and, as such, manifests itself by peculiar symptoms.

However it may be, a natural though perhaps morbid desire of submitting the case to the English-reading public was the consequence of those exceedingly brief and abortive polemics.

The Author was already engaged in the not over-congenial task of putting his own French into English, or what he hoped might do duty as such, when Messrs. George Routledge & Sons, the London publishers of his *Public Life in England*, kindly proposed to introduce *Ireland's Disease* to British society. The offer

Preface.

was heartily accepted, and so it came to pass that the English version is to appear in book form on the same day as the French one.

The special conditions of the case made it, of course, a duty to the author to strictly retain in his text every line that he had written down in the first instance, however little palatable it might prove to some English readers and fatal to his own literary or other prospects in England. That should be his excuse for sticking desperately to words which, like Tauchnitz editions, were not originally intended for circulation in Great Britain.

Ph. D.

Paris, *Nov.* 10*th*, 1887.

CONTENTS.

INTRODUCTION 1

CHAPTER I.
FIRST SENSATIONS 5

CHAPTER II.
DUBLIN LIFE 17

CHAPTER III.
THE POOR OF DUBLIN 31

CHAPTER IV.
THE EMERALD ISLE 46

CHAPTER V.
THE RACE 60

CHAPTER VI.
HISTORICAL GRIEVANCES 76

CHAPTER VII.
KILLARNEY 96

CHAPTER VIII.
THROUGH KERRY ON HORSEBACK 109

Contents.

CHAPTER IX.
A Kerry Farmer's Budget 139

CHAPTER X.
Rural Physiology 157

CHAPTER XI.
Emigration 177

CHAPTER XII.
The League 197

CHAPTER XIII.
The Clergy 215

CHAPTER XIV.
Fort Saunders 234

CHAPTER XV.
The Plan of Campaign 256

CHAPTER XVI.
Scottish Ireland 271

CHAPTER XVII.
Lex Licinia 296
   I.—The Gladstone Scheme 309
   II.—An Outsider's Suggestion 313

APPENDIX 331

IRELAND'S DISEASE.

INTRODUCTION.

It is indeed a chronic and constitutional disease that Ireland is labouring under. Twice within the last fifteen months it has been my fortune to visit the Sister Isle; first in the summer of 1886, at the apparently decisive hour when the die of her destiny was being cast in the ballot-box, and her children seemed on the point of starting upon a new life; then again, twelve months after, in the summer of 1887, when I found her a prey to the very same local disorders and to the same general anxiety that I had previously observed.

Last year it looked as if the solution was nigh, if Mr. Gladstone's spirited eloquence was going to carry the English nation along with it. The seasons, however, have followed one another in due course, bringing with them the usual run of unpaid rent, eviction, and reciprocal violence; a new Crimes Act has been added to the long record of similar measures that the British Parliament has scored against Ireland in eighty-seven years of so-called Union; a few cabins have disappeared, have been unroofed or burnt down by the arm of the bailiff; a few more skulls have been broken; some hundred thousand more wretched beings have embarked in emigrant ships for the United States or Queensland; some more hunger-stricken women and children have swollen the list of obscure victims that green Erin annually pays to the Anglo-Saxon Minotaur. But nothing essential is altered. Things are in the same places and passions at the same pitch. The two nations are facing each other with defiance in their eyes, threats in their mouths, revolvers or dynamite in hand. The problem has not advanced one step. Social war is still there, filling the hearts, paralysing the action, poisoning the springs of life. It may be read in the alarmed looks of mothers, in the sullen faces of men; it is lurking behind every hedge.

Before such an unparalleled case of a whole race's physiological misery, how could one help being seized with an ardent curiosity mingled with pity? Who would not wish to plunge to the bottom of the matter,

Introduction.

to make out, if possible, the secret of the evil, to deduce from it a lesson, and, may be, a general law?

That want I have felt most deeply, and I have tried to gratify it by personal observation; looking at things through my own spectacles, without animus or hatred, passion or prejudice, as they came under my gaze; noting down what seemed to be characteristic; above all, avoiding like poison the contact of the professional politician on either side: then drawing my own conclusion.

I need hardly add that for the intelligence of what I saw, I have always availed myself of the printed sources of information, such as the standard works on Irish history, Black's excellent *Guide to Ireland*, the Parliamentary Reports, the national literature, and last but not least the graphic accounts of current events published by the English and native press. Of the *Pall Mall Gazette*, especially, I must state that I have found its files a mine of precise, well digested, and thoroughly reliable information on the subject.

That my studies are above correction, I will not venture to hope. That they are in every case founded on facts, and, to the best of my belief, accurate, I earnestly vouch. As far as possible, I have made a point of giving the names of the persons mentioned. When it might have been inconvenient to them, however, or when delicacy forbade such a liberty, I have either suppressed the name or substituted a fictitious one. It should be understood that what I wanted, as a total stranger in the country, and what my French readers wanted, were not personal but typical instances.

CHAPTER I.

FIRST SENSATIONS.

DUBLIN.

HARDLY have you set foot on the quay at Kingstown, than you feel on an altogether different ground from England. Between Dover and Calais the contrast is not more striking. Kingstown is a pretty little place, whose harbour is used by the steamers from Holyhead, and whither Dublin shopkeepers resort in summer. Half a century back, it was only a fishermen's village of the most rudimentary description. But George IV., late Prince Regent, having done that promontory the honour to embark there when leaving Ireland, the place became the fashion. In memory of the glorious event, the citizens of Dublin raised on that spot a pyramid which rests on four cannon balls, and bears on its top the royal crown with the names of all the engineers, architects, captains, and harbour officials who had anything to do with the business. Villas soon sprang up round it, and from that time Kingstown went on thriving. A splendid pier bent round upon itself like a forearm on its humerus, makes it the safest harbour in Ireland, and the railway puts it in communication with Dublin in twenty minutes. It is the Portici of a bay that could vie with the Bay of Naples, did it boast its Vesuvius and sun, and did not the shoals which form its bottom get often bare and dry at low tide.

You land then at Kingstown, early in the morning after a four hours' crossing, having started the evening before by the express from Euston Station. And immediately you feel that you are no longer in England. The language is the same, no doubt, though talked with a peculiar accent or *brogue*. The custom-house officers are English; so are the policemen and red-coats who air themselves on the quay; but the general type is no longer English, and the manners are still less so. Loud talk, violent gesticulation, jokes and laughter everywhere; brown hair, sparkling dark eyes: you could imagine you are at Bordeaux or at Nantes.

The guard who asks for your ticket, the very train you get in, have something peculiar, undefinable, thoroughly un-English. The old lame newspaper-man who hands you *The Irish Times* or the *Freeman's Journal* at the carriage-door, indulges witticisms while giving you back your change, which not one of Mr. Smith's well-conducted lads ever permits himself along a British line. As for the passengers they are more un-English than anything else. This lady with the olive complexion and brown hair, may be termed an English subject; but for all that she has not probably one globule of Anglo-Saxon blood in her veins. That gentleman in the grey suit has evidently an English tailor, but the flesh-and-bone lining of his coat is of an altogether different make. As for the little man in black who is curling himself cosily in the corner opposite to you, not only is he unmistakeably a Roman Catholic priest, but you must positively hear him talk, to give up the idea that he is a Breton just out of the Saint Brieux Seminary. High cheek-bones, bilious complexion, small tobacco-coloured eyes, lank hair, nothing is missing from the likeness.

Here is Dublin. The train takes us to the very heart of the town, and there stops between a pretty public garden and the banks of the Liffey. The weather is cool and clear. Inside the station cabs and cars are waiting for travellers and their luggage. *Waiting*, not contending eagerly for their patronage as they do in London, where any possible customer is quickly surrounded by half-a-dozen rival drivers. "*Hansom, sir? . . . Hansom, sir?*" The Dublin cabman is more indolent. He keeps dozing on his seat or leisurely gossiping with his mates. "Why trouble oneself for nothing? The traveller knows how to call for a cab, I suppose!" So speaks the whole attitude of these philosophers in the Billycock hats.

This, however, will not prevent their being as unscrupulous as any of their fellow-drivers in any part of the globe, when it comes to settling the fare. "How much?" "Five bob." On verification you find that two shillings is all the rogue is entitled to. You give the two shillings, he pockets them and rattles away laughing. The job was a failure; no more.

Dublin is a big city, thickly populated, crossed by wide thoroughfares, provided with fine public gardens and splendid parks, which are here called *greens*, and adorned with an extraordinary number of statues. Its traffic and industry are important: visibly, this is a capital. More than a capital; the focus of a nationality. Everything in the streets proclaims it: sign-boards, monuments, countenances, manners. Those marble statues you see at every step are the effigies of the patriots who fought for the rights of Ireland. That palace with the noble colonnade, in the heart and finest part of the town, is the very building where the Irish Parliament, abolished in 1800 by the Act of Union, held its assemblies. Now-a-days the Bank directors meet in the room where once met the representatives of the nation. But they seem to have been careful not to change anything in the general arrangement, in case it was wanted to-morrow for some *Assemblée Constituante.* You may enter it : the door is open for every one. On the right you see what was the House of Lords, a rectangular hall with an open ceiling, historic hangings, and the statue of some royalties. On the left, the House of Commons. Here, mahogany counters stand in place of the members benches, and where sounded once the clash of argument, you hear now the tinkling of gold coins.

Let old times come again ; let Westminster give back to the Sister-Isle the autonomy she mourns, and, as a stage machinery, the Bank will vanish before the Parliament. It will be an affair of a night's work for the upholsterers.

In front of that building, which is the City Hall, it is not the British flag (though perhaps the law should insist upon it) that is hanging aloft. It is the green flag of Erin with the harp and the three towers. Everywhere there are calls on the national feeling. *Hibernian House, Hibernian Hotel, Erin Stores, Irish poplins*, *Irish gloves*, *Irish whisky*. Above all Irish whisky! one could not get comfortably drunk with Scotch whisky, that is evident.

If you visit a museum or picture-gallery you will find Art exiled in the background, and patriotism shining to the fore. Bating a fine Giorgione, a valuable Potter, a Van Steen of large size and extraordinary quality, a rare Cornelius Béga and a few others, the collection is not worth much, and would not fetch its million francs at the *Hotel des Ventes*, in the Rue Drouot. It is only a pretext for a national collection of portraits where are represented all the glories of Ireland, from Jonathan Swift, Laurence Sterne, Steele, Sheridan, Edmund Burke to Moore, Lord Edward Fitzgerald, the Duke of Wellington, and above all, O'Connell, "the liberator;" and Henry Grattan, esquire, "true representative of the people, father of liberty, author of the emancipation."

Those things take hold of you as soon as you arrive at Dublin. Like a flash of lightning they bring light upon many things about *Home Rule* which had remained hazy to your continental heedlessness. A nation with such memories kept up with such jealous care must know what it wants, and will have it in the end. Such signs are the manifestation of a national soul, of a distinct personality in the great human family. When all, from alderman to beggar, have one sole aim, they are bound to reach it sooner or later. Here, if the Town Hall has its green flag, the urchin in the street has his sugar-plum, shaped into the effigy of Parnell or Gladstone. Never, since the Venice and the Lombardy of 1859, was there such a passionate outburst of national feeling.

In the central part of the town, several streets are really fine with their rows of large houses, their gorgeous shops and numberless statues. The women are generally good-looking; well built, well gloved, well shod. They move gracefully, and with a vivacity which is quite southern. They look gentle and modest, and dress almost as well as Frenchwomen, of whom they have the quiet grace. The youngest ones wear their brown hair floating behind, and that hair, fine in the extreme, made more supple by the moistness of an insular climate, is crossed now and then by a most lovely glimmer of golden light.

Most of the men have acquired the significant habit of carrying large knotty cudgels in place of walking sticks. Other signs show a state of latent crisis, a sort of momentary truce between classes: for instance, the abundance of personal weapons, pneumatic rifles, pocket revolvers, &c., which are to be seen in the armourers' shop windows.

But what gives the principal streets of Dublin their peculiar character is the perpetual presence at every hour of the day of long rows of loiterers, which only one word could describe, and that is *lazzaroni*. As in Naples they stop there by hundreds; some in a sitting posture, or stretched at full length on the bare stone, others standing with their backs to the wall, all staring vaguely in front of them, doing nothing, hardly saying more, mesmerised by a sort of passive contemplation, and absorbed in the dull voluptuousness of inaction.

What do they live upon? When do they eat? Where do they sleep? Mystery. They probably accept now and then some occasional job which may bring them a sixpence. At such times they disappear and are mixed among the laborious population; you don't notice them. But their normal function is to be idle, to hem as a human fringe the public monuments.

Some places they seem to affect particularly; Nelson's Pillar amongst others. Whenever you pass it you are sure to see four rows of loungers seated on the pedestal, with legs dangling, pressed against each other like sardines.

Numerous tramcars, light and quick, cross Dublin in all directions. Five or six railway stations are the heads of so many iron lines radiating fan-wise over Ireland. All bear their national stamp; but what possesses that character in the highest degree is that airy vehicle called a jaunting-car.

Imagine a pleasure car where the seats, instead of being perpendicular to the shafts, are parallel with them, disposed back to back and perched on two very high wheels. You climb to your place under difficulties; then the driver seated sideways like you (unless the number of travellers obliges him to assume the rational position), lashes his horse, which plunges straightway into a mad career.

This style of locomotion rather startles you at first, not only on account of its novelty, but also by reason of the indifferent equilibrium you are able to maintain. Jostled over the pavement, threatened every moment to see yourself projected into space, at a tangent, you involuntarily grasp the nickel handle which is there for that purpose, just as a tyro horseman instinctively clutches the mane of his steed. But one gets used in time to the Irish car, and even comes to like it. First, it goes at breakneck speed, which is not without its charm; then you have no time to be bored, considering that the care of preserving your neck gives you plenty of occupation; lastly, you have the satisfaction of facing constantly the shop windows and foot paths against which you are likely to be tossed at any moment. Those are serious advantages, which other countries' cabs do not offer. To be candid, they are unaccompanied by other merits.

In that equipage you go to the Phœnix Park, the Dublin "Bois de Boulogne." It is a wide timbered expanse of some two thousand acres, full of tame deer, where all that is young in the place may be seen flirting, cricketing, playing all sorts of games, but above all, bicycling. Bicycles seem to be the ruling passion of the Dublin youth. I have seen more than a hundred at a time in a single lane near the Wellington Obelisk. By the way, this was the very avenue where Lord Frederick Cavendish and Mr. Burke were murdered five years ago by the *Invincibles*. A cross marks the place where the two corpses were discovered.

The Castle, which the two English officials had the imprudence to leave that day, is the Lord-Lieutenant's official residence. It has not the picturesque majesty of the castles of Edinburgh or Stirling.

Instead of rising proudly on some cloud-ascending rock and lording over the town, it seems to hide "its diminished head" under a little hillock in the central quarters. You must literally stumble over its walls to become aware of their existence; and you understand then why the name of *Dublin Castle* is for the Irish synonymous with despotism and oppression.

This is no Government office of the ordinary type, the dwelling of the Lord-Lieutenant of Ireland is a regular stronghold, encircled with ramparts, bristling with towers, shut up with portcullis, draw-bridge and iron bars. In the inner Castle yard are situated the apartments of the pro-consul, the lodgings of his dependants of all degrees, the offices where decrees are engrossed, the pigeon-holes where they are heaped, all forming a sort of separate city entrenched within its fortifications.

A very gem is the Royal Chapel, with its marvellous oak wainscoting, which twenty generations of carvers have concurred to elaborate. The reception-rooms, the hall of the Order of St. Patrick, where *drawing-rooms* are held, form the kernel of the fortress.

The barracks of the English soldiers and of those giant constables whom you see about the town are also fortified with walls, and form a line of detached forts round the central stronghold.

England is encamped at Dublin, with loaded guns and levelled rifles, even as she is encamped at Gibraltar, in Egypt, and in India.

CHAPTER II.

DUBLIN LIFE.

As there is little aristocracy in Dublin there are few lordly dwellings besides the Vice-regal castle. This is very striking in this country of lords and serfs. The masters of the land, mostly of English origin, do not care at all to live in the capital of Ireland; all the time that they do not spend on their property they prefer to beguile away in London, Paris, Naples or elsewhere. Few of their tradesmen are Irish; and the greatest part of the rents they raise on their lands merely accumulate in the banks of Dublin to be afterwards spent on the foreign markets. Thence this consequence, which explains many things:—The clearest of the nett product of the country's one industry — agricultural industry,— is poured outside it every year, without having circulated in Ireland, without having strengthened the local commerce or even invigorated agriculture itself, without having contributed to the well-being of a single

Irishman. Let us set down this nett product, the Irish aggregate rental, at its lowest estimate, £8,000,000 per annum, a sum much inferior to the nominal one, and admit that one-half of it is sent abroad to absentee landlords. There we have £4,000,000 leaving the island every year without conferring the slightest benefit to any one of its inhabitants. In ten years' time that represents 40 millions sterling; in fifty years, 200 millions sterling, or five milliards francs, that Ireland has, so to speak, thrown into the sea, for that is to her the precise equivalent of such a continuous deperdition of capital. . . . And this has lasted for three centuries ! . . . * What country would not be worn threadbare by such usage ? What nation could resist it ? Which individual, submitting to such periodical blood-lettings, would not succumb to anæmia ?

This anæmia betrays itself, even in Dublin, by many a symptom. For example, it is not long before one discovers that the finest shops, in the seven or eight principal streets, are a mere empty pretence ; great windows displaying all the wares possessed by the

---

* Absenteeism, in its present form, seems to date only from Grattan's Parliament, but in some shape or another it may be said to date from the British invasion of Ireland, and to result from the very nature of an insular kingdom transferred wholesale to the nobility of a neighbouring state.

merchant and beyond which the stock is *nil*. Money is so scarce that if you want to exchange a five pound note, in nine cases out of ten you do not get your right amount of change in specie. They give you back a quantity of small Irish banknotes, plus the change in half-crowns and shillings, and that not without having caused you to wait a long time while the important transaction was entered in and brought to a termination, and then only by the united energies of half the neighbourhood.

There is not in all the city one tolerable *restaurant* or *café* where a stranger can read the papers or obtain a decent beefsteak. The two or three pretentious taverns that aspire to fulfil that purpose are horrible dens, where, without the civilized accompaniment of napkins, they give you slices of cow, tough as leather, which are charged for at Bignon's prices.

Necessity compels you to fall back on the hotels, where they pitilessly give you the same fare night after night,—salmon and roast beef. The first day this can be borne, for the Shannon salmon deserves its reputation; the second day one begins to find it indigestible; the third, one would like to see all the salmon of Ireland choking the head waiter. The fourth, one takes the train rather than remain any longer exposed to this implacable fare. . . . Vain hope! it pursues you everywhere: on the shores of Kingstown or those of Blackrock, in the pretty town of Bray, or at the furthermost end of Wicklow's lakes. It is impossible to travel in Ireland without taking a dislike to salmon that will last the term of your natural life.

And yet the fresh herrings of the Bay of Dublin are eating fit for the gods, and the good wives sell them in the streets at three a penny. Do not hope to taste them, however, unless you do your own marketing, and insist, with conditional threats, upon having your herrings brought up for breakfast. You will have a fight to sustain; you will run the risk of appearing in the eyes of the waiter as a man of no breeding, one who does not shrink from exhibiting his morbid tastes to the public view. But your pains and your humiliations will be rewarded by such a dish as is not often to be met with in this vale of tears and bad cooking.

Dublin possesses three theatres, not including the future Opera-House, for which a site has already been chosen. The Gaiety, the most elegant of the three, gives musical burlesques that are rather entertaining, though they come straight from London.

But they are acted by Irishmen and Irishwomen, with all the dash, the brilliancy, the wit of the Celt. The comic actor of the company neglects nothing to amuse his audience; extravagant costumes, insane grimaces, jigs danced in brogues, impromptu verses on the events of the day,—he has any number of tricks at his command. That gentleman would score a sure success at the *Concert des Ambassadeurs*, with the ditty that actually delights the hearts of the Dublin public—"*That's all;*" it is about as stupid as the general literature of the Champs Elysées. The accomplished and fascinating *corps de ballet* exhibit tights of such indiscretion as the Lord Chamberlain would assuredly not tolerate in London. Is it that his jurisdiction does not extend to the sister isle; or does the thing which would imperil the virtue of club-loungers in Pall Mall appear to him without danger for those of Kildare Street? The problem would be worth studying. However that be, a boxfull of young officers in H. B. M.'s service seem greatly exhilarated by the display of ankles of the ladies, unless it be by the port wine of the mess.

These officers, in plain clothes as they are always when out of duty, are nevertheless easy to recognise, and seem about the only *swells* visible in the boxes.

The rest of the audience manifestly belong to the commercial and working classes.

For it is a fact that there is in Dublin no more upper middle class than there is aristocracy. The upper middle class seem not to exist, or to be only represented by tradespeople, the liberal professions, or the students. But these young men being, after the excellent English custom, lodged at the University, do not count in the pleasure-seeking public. In other words, they spend the evening in their rooms drinking toddy, instead of spending it, as with us, drinking small-beer in *brasseries*.

The University of Dublin, or rather, to speak more exactly, Trinity College, rises opposite Grattan's Parliament, in the very heart of the town. It is an agglomeration of buildings of sufficiently good style, separated by spacious courts, and surrounded by about thirty acres of ground planted with ancient trees. Technical museums, lecture-rooms, refectories, rooms for the Fellows and the pupils are all to be found there. There is a Section of Theology, one for Letters and Science, a Musical Section, a School of Medicine, a Law School, an Engineering School. Students and Masters all wear, as in Oxford or Cambridge, the stuff gown and the kind of black *Schapska*, which is the University head-covering throughout the United Kingdom.

Thinking of this, why is it we see so many Eastern head-dresses in the school of the west? With us the cap of the professors is the same that Russian popes wear. The Anglo-Saxons take theirs from Polish Lancers. That is an anomaly in the history of dress which ought to attract the meditations of academies.

Another anomaly, peculiar to Trinity College, is that the porters (most polite and benevolent of men) are provided with black velvet jockey caps, like the Yeomen of the Queen. They take the visitors through the museums of the place, and show them the plaster cast taken from the dead face of Swift, the harp of Brian Boru, and other relics of a more or less authentic character. The Dining Hall is ornamented with full-length portraits of the local celebrities. The library, one of the finest in the world, is proud of possessing, among many other riches, the manuscript (in the Erse tongue), of the "Seven times fifty Stories," which the bards of the Second Order of Druids used to recite, on ancient feast days, before the assembled kings and chieftains. Those venerable tales are subdivided into Destructions, Massacres, Battles,

Invasions, Sieges, Pillages, Raids of Cattle, Rapes of Women, Loves, Marriages, Exiles, Navigations, Marches, Voyages, Grottoes, Visions, Pomps, and Tragedies. This shows that "documentary literature" was not invented yesterday: all the primitive life of Celtic Ireland is told there.

The undergraduates at Trinity College do not seem, as a rule, like those of Oxford and Cambridge, to belong to the privileged or unoccupied classes. They are embryo doctors, professors, or engineers, who work with all their might to gain one of the numerous scholarships given by competition at the University. These competitions evidently excite an ardent emulation. I chanced to pass before the Examination Hall at the moment when the Rector at the top of the steps proclaimed the name of the candidate who had just won the Fellowship. Five hundred students at least, grouped at the gate, had been waiting for an hour to hear it, and saluted it with frantic cheers.

The Fellowship gives a right to board and lodging for seven years, with a stipend of some £400. It is a kind of prebend that implies few duties and leaves the titulary free to give himself up to his favourite studies. It has been the fashion in a certain set in France to go into ecstasies over this institution, and to regret that it should not have entered our own customs. The life of a Fellow at Oxford, Cambridge, or Dublin, was fondly represented to us as an ideal existence, freed from material cares, devoted exclusively to the culture of the mind. If we look at things more closely, we shall see that this opinion is wide of the mark. We find some of the prebendaries poorly lodged enough, submitted, by the exigencies of life in a community, to many a puerile rule, imprisoned within the narrow circle of scholastic ideas, and in too many cases buried up to the eyes in the sands of routine, if not in sloth, or drunkenness.

After all, for what strong, manly work is the world indebted to these much-praised Fellows? . . . The true effort of science or letters was never brought forth in these abbeys of Thelema of pedantry. Indeed it is much sooner born of individual struggle and large contact with the outside world. Even in the English Universities there is now a marked tendency to demand from the Fellow a work of positive utility in exchange for his salary. He must take his part in educating the pupils, help in the examinations, and in elaborating programmes; his life is much the same as that of our *Agrégés de Facultés*, with a something in it of lesser freedom and a semi-priestly character, if he be a bachelor. But he is free to marry now, and has been for a few years, on condition that he lives outside the college buildings.

The students, fourteen hundred in number, live two by two, in rooms of extreme simplicity, which they are at liberty to decorate according to their taste or means, with carpets, prints, and flowers. The names of the occupants are written over each door. The rooms generally include a small ante-chamber and a closet with glass doors. Women of venerable age and extraordinary ugliness are charged with the care of those young Cenobites' abode.

Trinity College was founded by Queen Elizabeth when she undertook the task of Anglicizing Ireland, and it has remained to our own day one of the strongholds of the conquering race. It is only since the year 1873 that the chairs and offices of this University have been accessible to Roman Catholics. Up to that time they were exclusively reserved for Anglicans, and Mr. Matthew Arnold would exclaim with good reason that such a state of things was the most scandalous in Europe. In France, he said, Protestant masters occupied all the chairs to which their merits entitled them; in Germany, Catholic professors taught history or philosophy at Bonn and elsewhere; while, in Catholic Ireland, the one University the country possessed remained closed during two centuries to all students that were not of the Protestant persuasion, and for three-quarters of the present century a Catholic could neither attain to a chair or to any degree of influence in it.

It was in the year 1845 that the movement began which was to triumph definitely in 1873, under the initiative of Mr. Gladstone. A certain Mr. Denis Caulfield Heron went up in that year for the competition for a fellowship, and took the first place. When he was, according to custom, invited to sign the Thirty-Nine Articles and to communicate in the University chapel, he opposed an absolute refusal, declaring himself to be a Roman Catholic; whereupon he was disqualified by the University Council. Mr. Heron exposed this judgment before the public, and succeeded in winning opinion to his side. But it proved an impossibility to make the Council recall their decision. The only thing Mr. Heron obtained, after a protracted struggle, was the creation of a new class of fellowships, accessible to Roman Catholics.

Finally, in 1873 the College authorities at last made up their minds to render the offices and emoluments of the University independent of any sectarian denomination ; nevertheless the Anglican spirit remains alive within its precincts, and manifests itself in the clearest manner upon occasions.

Intellectual life is alive in Dublin, as many a learned or literary society, a flourishing review, four great daily and several weekly papers, can testify. The daily papers especially are edited with a spirit and humour truly characteristic. It is a well known fact that the Sister Isle contributes a third at least to the recruiting of the Anglo-Saxon press, not only in Great Britain, but in the United States, in Australia, and in the whole of the English speaking world. The Irishman is a writer or a soldier born, as the Englishman is a born shopkeeper. The consequence is that the great papers in Dublin, the *Freeman's Journal*, the *Irish Times*, *United Ireland*, the *Express*, the *Evening Telegraph*, are admirably edited each in its own line.

But the same thing can hardly be said of the illustrated and coloured sheets that accompany the weeklies, and which are placarded everywhere. Those prints, bearing upon the political topics of the day, may possess the merit of teaching the crowd the lesson to be drawn from events; but they are lamentably inefficient from an artistic point of view.

Ireland, decidedly, shines no more than does our own Brittany in the plastic arts. Her best painter has been Maclise, and he is by no means a great master. However, her coloured prints delight the hearts of the good people of Dublin. An old newspaper-seller, smoking her pipe at the corner of Leinster Street, holds her sides for very laughter as she contemplates the cartoon given this day by the *Weekly News;* it represents a mob of Orangemen in the act of pelting the Queen's police with stones at Belfast. Underneath run the words: "*Behold loyal Ulster!*"

The quays of the Liffey are lined with book-shops like those of the Seine in Paris, to which they present a certain likeness. Following the quays from the west, one passes the building where sit the four Supreme Courts—Chancery, Exchequer, Queen's Bench, and Common Pleas. The statues of Faith, Justice, Wisdom, and Piety rise under its Corinthian peristyle, which caused the typical Irish peasant, the Paddy of legend, to exclaim:

"They did well to place them outside, for no one will ever meet them inside!"

The judges, chosen by the Queen's government, bear the title of *Chief Justice* or *Baron*. There are four at each tribunal, each provided with a salary ranging from three to eight thousand pounds a year. They sit in groups of three, bewigged and clad in violet gowns, with peach-coloured facings, at the extremity of a recess screened by red curtains. Before them sit the barristers and clerks in black gowns and horsehair wigs. The writs and briefs of procedure, written out upon awe-inspiring sheets of foolscap paper, are piled up within capacious green bags, such as are only seen with us at the Comédie Française when they play *Les Plaideurs*. The judges appear to be a prey to overwhelming *ennui*, so do the barristers. The public, not being paid as highly as they are for remaining in this sleepy atmosphere, keep constantly going in and out. Now and then, however, Irish wit must have its due: some one delivers himself of a spicy remark; everyone wakes up a bit to laugh, after which business quietly resumes its dull course.

CHAPTER III.

THE POOR OF DUBLIN.

PRIVATE houses are built in Dublin on the general type adopted throughout the British Isles: a basement opening on the railed area which runs along the pavement, a ground floor, a first floor, sometimes a second one. Above the front door a pane of glass lighted with gas. It is the custom of the country to place there one's artistic treasures,—a china vase, a bust, or a small plaster horse. The small horse especially is a great favourite. You see it in a thousand copies which all came out of the same cast. In the suburbs you notice pretty often a window decorated with plants that are seen behind the glass panes,— Breton fashion,—and, striking circumstance, in Ireland also it is the uninteresting geranium which is the favourite flower of the poor. Inside the house the accommodation is nearly the same as in England. It is well known that nothing is more like an English house than another English house. But here, to the classical furniture, horse-hair and mahogany armchairs, and oil-cloth floor, is added a mural decoration of coloured prints and Roman Catholic chromolithographs, Saint Patrick, the Pope Leo XIII., the "Good Shepherd giving His life for the sheep," surrounded by dried branches of holy palm, rosaries and scapularies. An ornament greatly appreciated on the chimney-piece is a glass vessel full of miraculous water in which swims a reduction of the tools of the Passion, the cross, the ladder, the hammer, the nails, and the crown of thorns.

Eighty-seven per cent. of the Dublin population belong to the Roman Catholic religion. The proportion is higher in some other Irish counties : in Connaught it rises to ninety-five per cent. ; nowhere, even in Protestant Ulster, does it descend lower than forty-five per cent.

And those Catholics are not so only in name. The greater number follow the services of the Church, observe all the rites, maintain a direct and constant intercourse with the priests. The sincerity of their faith is particularly striking, and is not to be found in the same degree even in Italy or in Spain. For with them the Roman faith is narrowly bound with traditions most dear to their race ; it remains one of the external forms of protestation against the conquest, and has been, till quite lately, a stigma of political incapacity. To the glamour of the traditional religion is added the poetry of persecution and the rancour of the vanquished. This religion is the one that is not professed by the hated Englishman: what a reason to love it above all the others! We must remember that in Dublin, amidst a population nine-tenths of which are devout Catholics, and where the remaining tenth is alone Protestant (Episcopalian' Presbyterian, Methodist, &c.), the cathedral is in the hands of the Anglican minority with all the ancient basilics, whilst the worship of the majority is sheltered in modern and vulgar buildings. The conquering race has invaded Saint Patrick's Baptistery as well as the Royal Castle, and the Senate of the University. A threefold reason for rancour to these who were thus deprived of the three sanctuaries of faith, public power, and learning.

Such spoliations are those which a vanquished race cannot forget, because they bring constantly their sore under their eyes. Now the Irish have the artless vanity of the chivalrous races, and the wounds inflicted to their self-love are perhaps more cruel than the others.

This vanity is frequently exhibited in a certain taste for show, and in a slight touch of the mountebank. The least apothecary's shop in Dublin goes by the pompous name of *Medical Hall;* the smallest free school is an academy; and it is well known that every single Irishman is descended straight from the " ould kings of Oireland."

There is a great deal of misery in Dublin; 6,036 of her inhabitants are inmates of the workhouse; 4,281 are the recipients of outdoor relief; 19,332 are without a known trade or profession and without means of living. It makes about 30,000 paupers in a town of 250,000 inhabitants. Besides those officially recognised paupers, how many others whose distress is no less terrible for not being classed!

I had the first sight of that misery on the quay of the Liffey. It was a dishevelled woman walking as in a trance, her eyes settled, immoveable. Barefooted, dressed in a yellowish tattered shawl which hardly covered her withered breast, and in a horrible nondescript silk petticoat once black, through which her thighs appeared. She was pale and silent, and she seemed to be lost in some unutterable grief. I spoke to her—she did not answer. I put a piece of money in her hand, she took it without a word, without even looking at it. She went her way.

I thought I had seen the ghost of the *Shan Van Vocht*, "The Poor Old Woman," as the Irish sorrowfully call their country. She went with long strides towards the police court—a new building, not far from Richmond Bridge. I went in after her.

In the courtyard, groups of beings with human faces were crouching on the ground—so black, so dirty, so tattered were they, that they made me think of the Australian aborigines and Fuegian savages, of the most unenlightened and degraded tribes of the globe. Most of them bore outwardly the semblance of women. The males were standing with their backs against the wall in that listless attitude of the "unemployed" in Dublin.

An ill-kept staircase leads to the audience room. The walls are whitewashed, the ceiling a skylight, white wooden benches round the room.

In the chair, the police judge; he is a yellow-haired man with a benevolent countenance, dressed in a frock coat. Clerks and counsel are alike gownless and wigless; everything is conducted in a homely manner. The accused follow each other in single file. The witness (nearly always a constable) states what he has seen. The judge asks the delinquent if he has anything to say in his defence, and after a quick colloquy he pronounces his sentence. Generally it is a fine of two or three shillings or a day's imprisonment for each unpaid shilling.

One of the prisoners has just been condemned to pay a fine of half a crown for obvious drunkenness; he does not possess a farthing, but seems to be endowed with a humorous turn of mind.

"Your honour could as well have said half a sovereign! It would have looked more respectable, and the result would have been the same," he says, turning his pockets inside out. A guffaw of laughter joined in by the judge himself, who does not think it his duty to be offended by the remark; after which he calls out for number two.

Number two is a boy fifteen or sixteen years old; he has a sweet intelligent countenance in spite of the indescribable rags that cover his body. Tears stand in his eyes and his lips are tremulous. Nothing in him of the habitual offender. The accusation that he is lying under seems to be : " Theft of a pork-chop in an open shop-window." A single witness is called, a little maid five years old ; so small that her head does not even reach the top of the witness-box. They bring her a footstool, on which she climbs to give her evidence.

She has seen the boy, she says, near the shop window, looking wistfully for a long time on the chops and finally pocketing one. However, her account is not very clear. All those people make her shy, and she does not speak out loud, so the clerk takes the trouble to read over to her the evidence she has just given. Does she know how to write? Can she sign her name? Yes. They place a pen in her fingers, and with infinite trouble, bending her small fair head, shooting out her lips, she writes on the legal parchment with her tiny trembling hand her name and surname: *Maggie Flanagan.*

"Well! prisoner, what have you to say?"

The unfortunate boy stammers that he was hungry, that there was not a penny in the house, and that he had no work.

"What is your father's trade?"

"He is gone to Australia, your honour. Mother has been left with four children. I am the eldest. We had eaten nothing for two days."

One feels he is speaking the truth. Every heart is moved.

Suddenly a shrill voice bursts out from the lower

end of the room, wailing: "Oh, your honour, don't send him to jail! . . ."

It is the woman I saw on the quay; the one that I followed to that Purgatory. The mother of the culprit very likely.

"I am obliged to remand you for a week in order to examine the circumstances of the case," the judge says, in a manner that shows he is anxious to arrange the affair with kindness.

The prisoner goes out of the dock following the warder, and disappears through a small side door.

The mother has gone away without waiting, and I hurry to follow her. But she walks so fast that I can hardly keep pace with her.

She passes again on the bridge, walks along the quay, plunges in a by-street, goes up towards the south-western quarters of Dublin, called the *liberties* of the town. Suddenly I lose sight of her at the corner of a narrow lane, and after winding round and round I am obliged to renounce coming up with her. There is a way of course to come to the relief of those poor creatures, by sending one's subscription to the judge according to the British fashion. But I wanted to see them at home in their den, wallowing in their squalor, to see whether men or destiny bear the responsibility for such dark distress.

Alas! examples are not wanting, and I have only to cross the first door that opens before me. Along these lanes yawn dark alleys from which hundreds of half-naked children are swarming out. All ages are represented; they are in the most fantastical and unexpected attire. One has got on breeches fastened under the shoulders by a piece of cord in lieu of braces; the same is full of holes large enough for his head to go through. Another has no shirt, and trails in the gutter the jagged skirt of a coat slashed like a doublet, and with only one sleeve left. They are all of them so extravagantly slovenly that it seems to be a competition for rags.

A baby two or three years old strikes me particularly. It is absolutely naked, and so very, very dirty that dirt has formed a sort of bronzed skin over his little body, and he is like a juvenile nigger. As he came into the world so he has remained. Neither soap nor water ever moistened his skin. He has not even undergone the washing that the mother-cat applies so industriously with her tongue on her new-born kittens.

Yet his mother loves him, squalid and black as he is. Just now a cart passed, and the baby was running under the wheels; the mother sprang out of her lair with the roar of a tigress, and pounced upon her child, which she jealously carried away.

Never in London did I hear such accents. Far from me to hint that English mothers do not love their babies: but they love them after their own fashion, without showers of kisses or demonstrative ways.

And this is the distinctive feature which divides the Irish pariahs from those of the London East-End. They love each other, and they know how to put that love into words. Their distress, perhaps deeper than English poverty, bears not the same hard, selfish character—tenderness and love are not unknown to them. They try to help and comfort one another in their misery. Thackeray has remarked it long ago: let an Irishman be as poor as you like; he will always contrive to find another Irishman poorer still, whom he will serve and oblige, and make the partaker of his good or bad luck. And it is absolutely true. That fraternal instinct, so unknown to the Anglo-Saxon, nay, so contrary to his nature, shows itself here at every step.

But the misery is none the less terrible here; indeed, there are no adequate words in the dictionary to express it. No description can give an idea of those nameless dens, sordid, dilapidated stairs, miserable pieces of furniture, nondescript utensils invariably diverted from their original destination. And in that lamentable frame, those swarming families squatting in their filth; the starved look of the mothers under the tattered shawl that ever covers their heads, the hungry little faces of their whelps . . . . . .

A sickening smell, recalling that of ill-ventilated hospitals, comes out of those lairs and suffocating you, almost throws you back. But it is too late. You have been caught sight of. From all sides visions of horror are emerging to light, spectres are starting up; old hags that would have surprised Shakespeare himself, swarm round you, holding out their hand for a *copper*. The younger women don't generally come to the front, not that their wants be less, but they know that coppers are not inexhaustible, and that the old ones must have the precedence. So they remain sadly in the background, and then, when you have emptied your pockets, there is a roar of benedictions fit to rend one's heart with shame. They are so fearfully sincere! And how many times do we not throw to the winds of our caprice what would be sufficient to quench at least for one moment, the thirst which is raging in that hell! You fly from that den of horror, wondering whether the most horrible deserts would not be more merciful to those destitute creatures than the *liberties* of the city of Dublin.

In your flight you fatally fall upon Nicholas Street, where all those dark alleys open. This is the way to the cathedral, and the great commercial artery of this side of the town. If any doubt remained in you after the insight you had of the houses of the poor in Dublin, about the way they live, that street alone would give you sufficient information.

From end to end it is lined with a row of disgusting shops or stalls, where the refuse of the new and the ancient world seems to have come for an exhibition. Imagine the most hideous, ragged, repulsive rubbish in the dust-bins of two capitals, and you will get an idea of that shop-window display; rank bacon, rotten fish, festering bones, potatoes in full germination, wormy fruit, dusty crusts, sheep's hearts, sausages which remind you of the Siege of Paris, and perhaps come from it; all that running in garlands or festoons in front of the stalls, or made into indescribable heaps, is doled out to the customers in diminutive half-pence morsels. At every turning of the street a public-house with its dim glass and sticky glutinous door. Now and then a pawnbroker with the three symbolic brass balls, and every twenty yards a rag and bone shop.

The rag and bone trade is extremely active in Dublin, which numbers no less than 400 shops of that description, according to statistics. And that is not too many for a population which from times immemorial never wore a garment that was not second-hand. To a man Ireland dresses on the *reach-me-down* system, and wears out the cast-off garments which have passed on the backs of ten or twelve successive owners. Battered hats, dilapidated gowns, threadbare coats arrive here by shiploads. When the whole world has had enough of them, when the Papoo savages and Guinea niggers have discarded their finery, and declared it to be no longer serviceable, there are still amateurs to be found for it in Dublin. Hence the most extraordinary variety, and the wildest incoherence of costume. Knee-breeches, tail coats, white gowns, cocked hats,—Paddy and his spouse are ready for anything. So destitute are they of personal property, that they do not even possess an outline of their own. Their normal get-up resembles a travesty, and their distress a carnival.

The main point for them is to have a garment of any description to put on, since it is a thing understood that one cannot go about naked; and it does not very much matter after all what is the state of that garment, as it is so soon to leave their backs to go to the pawnbroker's. This is a prominent figure in the daily drama of their wretched existence, the regulator of their humble exchequer through the coming and going of the necessaries of life, which they are obliged to part with periodically.

"You see that pair of hob-nailed shoes?" one of them tells me, "For the last six months it has come here every Monday regularly and gone every Saturday. The possessor uses them only on Sundays; on week days he prefers enjoying his capital . . ."

His capital!—one shilling and sixpence, for which he has to pay an interest of one penny a week; *i.e.*, three hundred per cent. a year!

Usury under all its forms blooms spontaneously on that dung-hill. By the side of the pawnbroker a *money office* is almost always to be seen. It is an English institution, natural in a nation which is bursting with money, and consequently finds it difficult to make it render 3 or 4 per cent. What is England if not a colossal bank, which advances money upon any three given signatures as a security, if they come from people with a settled dwelling and a regular profession? Well, who would believe it?

Paddy himself is admitted to partake of the onerous benefits of that credit, provided he work ever so little and be not too hopelessly worn out. For these small banking houses form a union and let each other know the state of their accounts. Upon the poor man's signature accompanied by those of two of his fellows, five and seven pounds sterling will be lent to him, to be reimbursed by weekly instalments. But that resource, which is a powerful help for the strong energetic man, is almost invariably a cause of distress and ruin to the weak. The borrowed money ebbs out in worthless expenditure, in the buying of some articles of apparel or furniture, which soon takes the road to the pawnbroker's; and the debt alone remains weighing with all its weight on poor Paddy. It is the last straw on the camel's back, and he ends by falling down irremediably under it.

CHAPTER IV.

THE EMERALD ISLE.

NOTHING can be easier than to go from one end to the other of Ireland. Though her network of railways is not yet complete, great arteries radiate from Dublin in all directions and allow the island to be traversed from end to end, whether southward, westward, or northward, in less than seven or eight hours. The journey from south to north, following the great axis, is longer and more complicated, for it is necessary to change lines several times. The circular journey along the coasts is facilitated by excellent services of open coaches, that go through the regions not yet penetrated by railways. Lastly, one can, by following the Shannon, enter by steamboat almost to the very heart of the country.

When one has gone through those various excursions, completed by riding and walking tours, and seen the island under its various aspects, one perceives that it presents in a general manner the appearance of a cup, with brims rising towards the sea; in other words, it consists in a vast central plain, protected on all its circumference by groups of hills and mountains, preventing the inroad of the ocean. Those mountains are in no part very high; the finest, those of Kerry, do not rise above 1800 feet. But their very position on the brink of the Atlantic, the erosions undermining their base, the deep bays they delineate, the innumerable lakes hidden away in their bosoms, lend them a majesty far above their altitude. Bland and smiling in Wicklow, they are in Kerry of an unequalled serenity, while in Connemara they preserve unbroken the rude chaos of primeval cataclysms, and display on the north of Antrim's table-land, towards the Giant's Causeway, the most stupendous basaltic formations.

Yet the normal, the truest aspect of Ireland, is represented by the central plain—a large, unbroken surface of green undulating waves, ever bathed in a damp and fresh atmosphere, shut in on the horizon by dark blue mountains.

This aspect is of infinite sweetness; no land possesses it in a similar degree. It takes possession of you, it penetrates you like a caress and a harmony. One understands, when submitted to that entirely physical influence, the passionate tenderness that

Irishmen feel for their country, and that is best illustrated by Moore's poetry. The sky seems to have endeavoured to find the true chord in response to the earth, in order to give to all things those deliciously blended tones. The stars are nearly always seen through a light haze, and the sun itself shines but through a veil of vapours, into which it seems eager to disappear again. The shadows are not hard and well defined; they melt into each other by insensible gradations of tint. All is green, even the stones, clothed in moss; the walls, covered with ivy; the waters, hidden under a mantle of reeds and waterlilies. In other climes the fields, after a spring shower, take unto themselves the bravery that here is seen in all seasons. In the full heat of July the corn, the barley, the oats still keep their April dress. Do they ever ripen? They say they do, towards the end of October; but surely they never can get yellow. Yellow is not an Irish colour, nor is white. Ireland is indeed green Erin, the Emerald Isle. Never was name more truly given.

One could consider Ireland as a prodigious grass plot of some twenty million acres, constantly watered by rain. Water is everywhere: in the clouds that the winds of the Atlantic drive over her, and that the highlands of Scotland and Norway stop in their course; on the soil, where all hollows, great or small, become lakes; under the ground even, where the roots of vegetables, saturated and swollen like sponges, slowly change into peat. Ireland is the most liberally watered country in Europe, and yet, thanks to the constancy of the winds over her, one can scarcely say it is a damp country. The fall of water is on an average of 926 millimetres in a year—a little over three feet. The ground, naturally of admirable fruitfulness, is still further favoured by the mildness and equableness of the climate on the shores.

The flora almost recalls that of the Mediterranean coasts. The fauna presents the remarkable peculiarity of not possessing a single dangerous or even repulsive species—not one toad, not one reptile, except the most innocent among them all, the "friend of man," the lizard. Legends say that St. Patrick, the Christian apostle of the isle, coming from Brittany in the 6th century, threw all the serpents into the sea, and all the toads after them; indeed, he is habitually represented in popular imagery as engaged in performing that miracle.

An island possessing no backbone, and presenting generally the appearance of a cup, cannot have great rivers. In fact, almost all the rivers of Ireland, born within her girdle of mountains, soon lose themselves in the sea, forming at their mouth an estuary that takes the name of *Lough*, as do the lakes proper. One only creates an exception by the length of its course and the volume of its waters—the Shannon, rising in the central table-land, imprisoned, so to speak, at the bottom of the circular well, and whose course, impeded above Limerick by a barrier of rocks, form fine rapids, under which the waters flow in a majestic stream. With the tide, vessels of the heaviest tonnage can go up the river to Foynes.

Indeed, the country lacks no harbours on those deeply indented shores. North, west, east, and south, Ireland counts no less than fourteen natural harbours, large enough to shelter whole fleets.

But this gift, like all the others that Fate has showered on her, seems to have turned against her by bringing the nations of prey within those bays. Thrown as an outwork of Europe in the middle of the ocean, she seemed to be opening her arms to the Phœnicians, to the Scandinavians; later on to the Arabs, the

Spaniards, and the English. A gust of wind was enough to reveal her to them ; a favourable breeze to bring them back. To understand clearly the perils of such a post, and to see how much more still than the muzzle of Brittany, Ireland is Atlantic land, one must go to Valencia, the small islet on which come to shore the ends of the Transatlantic cables.

More than in any other spot of Europe one feels at the farthest end of the world there. It seems as if, by stretching one's arm, one would reach the United States. And, in fact, one is near enough as it is— five or six days by steam—almost within speaking distance with the telephone. So fast travel the storms from America that the telegram is hardly able to arrive before them. A sea-gull, borne on the wing of the hurricane, would cross that arm of the sea in a few hours. The breeze that blows in your face may have stirred the hair of a Brooklyn belle in the morning. There one feels how very small is our globe.

Geologically, Ireland differs much from Great Britain. The island appeared much earlier, and its structure is special. Alone, its northern part, or Ulster, which, from a political point of view, forms such a striking contrast with the rest of the island, presents between Donegal Bay and Dundalk Bay, mountainous masses, entirely analogous with those of Scotland, towards which they advance, and of which they appear originally to have formed a part. They are basaltic rocks, or petrified streams of lava, while the mountains in Kerry or Connemara are red sandstone and slate, lying above the carbonaceous strata.

What ought, in fact, to be considered as Ireland proper consists, then, of the eastern province or Leinster, the southern or Munster, and the western or Connaught. Ulster is in reality, as well by the nature of its soil as by the race and habits of the majority of its inhabitants, an annex and dependency of Scotland. The three other provinces, on the contrary, form a whole, as distinct from England or Scotland by the constitution and aspect of the land, as it is different by the race, genius, the traditions and beliefs of the population.

The most striking thing on a first sight of the Irish landscape is the total absence of trees of any kind. They are only seen in private parks. As far as the eye can see the plains spread in gentle undulations, covered with grass and intersected with stone walls; no single oak, elm, or shrub ever comes to break its monotony. The tree has become a lordly ensign. Wherever one sees it one may be certain the landlord's mansion is not far.

That radical disappearance of the forests, in a country once covered with them, is singular. A great many explanations have been given of this fact,—explanations that went back as far as some geological cataclysm. Such theories are no longer acceptable in these days. The most likely supposition is that all the available timber has gradually been felled down for domestic uses, and that indifference, poverty, incessant war, incertitude as to the present or future, have, from the remotest times, prevented those sad gaps being repaired.

On the lower land the absence of timber is explained of itself by the apparition of deep layers of turf, whose depth is sometimes from forty-five to sixty feet, in which whole oak trees have been discovered in a more or less advanced state of carbonisation. At a certain stage of this transformation the ligneous tissue has become of such flexibility that the Irish cut it into stripes and use it to make straps, fishing nets, bands of all kinds,—not to mention the pious trifles, pipes, small figures carved with a knife, and various *souvenirs* with which they pester the tourist.

The turf pits are a great source of riches for Ireland, and furnish the only fuel commonly used by the lower classes. In the country one sees everywhere people engaged in extracting peat, cutting it into cakes, erecting these cakes in pyramids to be allowed to dry in the sun, or transporting them from one place to the other. The people working at it are, indeed, almost the only ones visible in the fields. One might think that the extracting and manipulating of the turf were the only industry of the country.

There are two kinds of turf, the red and the black, according to the degree of carbonisation attained by the layers, and the nature of the vegetable matter that formed them. The finest is of such intense and brilliant black, that it might almost be mistaken for coal. Those vast reservoirs of fuel, known in Ireland by the name of *bog*, are a constant feature of the landscape in the valleys of the mountainous girdle as in the lower parts of the plain. The total depth of these open carbon mines is estimated at no less than sixty million cubic feet; they occupy an area almost equal to the seventh part of the total superficies of the island, and the lakes cover another seventh part.

One other striking peculiarity of the scenery in Ireland is the scarcity of cultivated fields. One can count them, dotted here and there, almost always planted with oats, potatoes, or turnips. The statistics of the Agricultural Society give, in round numbers, for twenty millions of acres of total surface, five millions, or a quarter in cultivated ground; that is, 150,000 acres only in cereals, 350,000 in turnips, one million and a half in potatoes, two million in artificial meadows. Ten million of acres are in natural meadows; the rest are fallow lands, bog or turf, waste land, roads and highways.

Those roads and highways, as well as the bridges and all the public works depending upon the English Government, are admirably kept. It is clear that on that point Dublin Castle is resolved to give no handle to criticism. Those splendid tracks of road, laid across waste and desert land, even produce a curious effect, and one would be tempted to see an affectation about it, did they not, in the majority of cases, lead to some magnificent private property, spreading as far as one can see over hill and dale, always shut in by stone walls eight or ten feet high, enclosing an area of several miles.

As for the conveyances that are seen on these Appian Ways they are of two kinds; either the smart carriage whose cockaded coachman drives magnificent horses, or the diminutive cart drawn by a small donkey, carrying, besides the grand-dame or child that drives it, a sort of conical-shaped utensil held in its place with cords and oftener filled with water than with milk. One must go to Morocco or Spain to see donkeys in such numbers as in Ireland.

———————

One thing surprises in those endless pastures—it is to count so few grazing beasts on them. Not that they are altogether excluded; now and then one perceives on the intense green of the fields reddish or white spots that are cattle or sheep, the rounded haunch of a mare, the awkward frolics of a foal. On the brinks of rivers that one can almost always cross wading, one sometimes sees a few happy cows, their feet in the water, wide-eyed and munching dreamily. Here and there one sees geese, hens escorted by their chicks, pigs fraternally wallowing with children in the muddy ditch. But in a general way the landscape is wanting in animated life, and as poor in domestic animals as in labourers.

As a contrast game is plentiful, as is natural in a land that is three-quarters uncultivated, where it is forbidden to carry arms, and where shooting is the exclusive privilege of a very small minority. Hares and rabbits seem to enjoy their immunity to the utmost, and everywhere their white breeches are seen scudding away in the dewy grass like fireworks.

Villages are rare, and rarer still is farmhouse or homestead. Undulating ridges succeed to undulating ridges and still one sees no trace of any dwellings. One might think that these stone walls radiating over the fields had sprung there of their own accord, and that the hay is doomed to rot standing, after feeding the butterflies. Yet that cannot be—evidently some one must come now and then to cut this grass, make it into stacks and carry it away. . . . At last, by dint of stretching neck and legs you succeed in discovering far away on the horizon a spire that belongs to a big borough, a market-town rather, where those civic tillers of the soil dwell in houses similar to those of the *liberties* in Dublin.

As for the mud cabin, generally described as the Irish peasant's only home, it is now a thing of the past. One would hardly, and after much research, find some specimens of it in the farthest counties, at the end of Kerry or Mayo.

True to say, when found, those specimens leave nothing to be desired for poverty and discomfort; no fire-place, no windows, no furniture; nothing but a roof of turf supported by a few poles on mud walls. The very pig that formerly shared its luxuries with the *genus homo* and indicated a certain degree of relative comfort in his possessor, the pig himself has disappeared for ever.

But those are exceptions, almost pre-historic cases. As a rule the mud cabin has been blotted out from the Irish soil—perhaps enlightened landlords systematically pursued its eradication; perhaps the peasants, tired of its tutelary protection, emigrated under other skies,—or more simply still, they took advantage of the last famine to die of hunger. Upon which came the rain, and two or three years sufficed to dilute the walls, render the mud house to the common reservoir, and wash out its very remembrance.

The population of Ireland, it must be borne in mind, has been steadily decreasing for half a century.

The Emerald Isle.

It was of 8,175,124 inhabitants in 1841 ; of 6,552,385 in 1851 ; 5,798,584 in 1861 ; 5,412,377 in 1871 ; and 5,174,836 in 1881. By all appearances it must now have sunk under five millions. If this fish-eating race was not the most prolific under the sun it would have been blotted out long ago from the face of this planet.

CHAPTER V.

THE RACE.

The essential character of Irish scenery is, besides the green colour and the absence of trees, the frequent ruins that meet the eyes everywhere—one cannot go two steps without seeing them. Ruins of castles, abbeys, churches, or even humble private dwellings. There are quarters of large towns or boroughs, such as for instance the northern one in Galway, that might be taken at night, with their sinister looking rows of houses, roofless and with gaping walls, for a street in Herculaneum or Pompeii. When the ancient stone walls are those of a church or chapel, they generally serve as a setting for the legends of the country-side; there occurred all the terrifying tales of former days, there took place all the local miracles, and there still is the favourite haunt of illustrious spirits, of fairies and *banshee*.

Almost in every case the graves of a hamlet come to group themselves at the foot of those ivy-clothed old walls, by an instinctive and touching effect of the Irishman's passionate love for the traditions of his race ; and those graves, generally covered with great slabs of stone, scattered among the tall grasses, wild and moss-grown, without cross or emblem of any sort, well accord with the melancholy aspect of the site.

Sometimes near these ruins and graves is still seen, proudly raising its head, one of those monuments peculiar to the country and about which antiquaries are at such variance,—the round towers of Ireland: slender and bold turrets, slightly conical in shape, not unlike minarets 75 or 80 feet high, upon a base 15 to 18 feet broad, and springing from the ground like obelisks. They are built of large stones, sometimes rough, sometimes cut, but always cemented together, a fact which gave rise to the opinion that they must be posterior to the invasion of Great Britain by the Romans. But that is simply begging the question and is justified by nothing; moreover, the absence of any tradition about the origin or use of those towers make such a tale appear in the highest degree improbable. A race was never seen to borrow the technical industry of another race to apply it to the construction of monuments that are essentially their own. Celtic civilization had attained in Ireland, centuries before the Romans, to a degree of perfection witnessed by the Brehon Code, compiled at least five or six centuries before the Christian era, and the first among human laws that substituted arbitrage to brute force. A people capable of submitting to the law of reason and who knew enough of mechanics to erect monoliths of twenty-four thousand cubic feet could well discover alone the art of mixing mortar, and need not borrow it from the Romans, who besides did not set foot in the country. Never was hypothesis more childish or more unfounded. The truth is that nothing is known about the round towers, as is the case with the *nurraghs* of Sardinia; that all those monuments are anterior to any positive traditions and have been built for uses of which we have no conception. At the most one might suppose from their aspect, which is that of inland lighthouses, that they may have been used as military or astronomical observatories, and, perhaps, bore on their summit a sacred fire visible throughout a whole district. In such a case the only guide to be followed with any certainty is the eternal fitness between organ and function.

Eighty-three of these towers are still standing in Ireland, and their dilapidated condition allows it to be supposed that they may once have been much

The Race.

more numerous. Whatever may have been their origin, they remain so narrowly and so fitly associated in the popular imagination with the Irish idea of nationality that the image of a round tower naturally grew under the chisel of the sculptor, as an emblem of patriotism, on the tomb of O'Connell in the cemetery of Dublin.

Megalithic monuments and dolmen are equally found in great numbers in Ireland. Donegal presents at Raphre a circus of raised stones absolutely similar to that of Stonehenge, while in Derry one sees in the Grianan of Aileach the finest fortified temple that was ever raised in honour of the sun. In many districts all the hills or mountains without exception are crowned with the funeral hillock or Celtic *rath*. As for the Druidical inscriptions in the *Ogham* character, consisting of twenty-five combinations of oblique or vertical strokes corresponding to an equal number of sounds, they abound in all the counties. The most curious is that of the Cave of Dunloe, discovered by a labourer, in the vicinity of Killarney, in the year 1838 ; it may be considered a true Druidical library, of which the books are represented by the stones of the vaulted roof. Those characters have been deciphered now, thanks to bilingual inscriptions posterior to the Roman period.

Lastly, the names of places and the geographical definitions are, in nine cases out of ten, of Celtic origin, according to the tables drawn out by Chalmers. The mountains are called *ben*, and the chains of hills *sliebh*, rocks are *carricks* or *cloagh*, lakes *loughs*, an island *innis*, bogs *corks*, lands *curraghs*, hills *knocks*, rivers *anagh*.

The Erse tongue, still spoken by a twelfth part of the population, is sister to the Gaelic and the Breton. It denominates a field *agh*, a ford *ath*, a village *bally*, a city *cahir*, *ban* what is white or beautiful, *deargh* what is red, *dua* what is black, *beg* what is small, and *mor* what is big, *clar* a plain, *teach* a house, *donagh* a church, *ross* a wooded hillside.

As for the type of the Irish race it is undeniably Celtic, or at least essentially different from the Anglo-Saxon. The hair is black or brown, the eyes dark, the complexion pale, the nose short, the forehead bony. The general appearance is vigorous and active, the movements are quick and often graceful; the stature without being low, is nearer to middle height than is generally the case in a British country. The rudest peasant girls often have a sculptural grace of attitude; one sees them in the fields, carrying burdens on their head with that stateliness of Greek canephores which seems as a rule the exclusive attribute of the daughters of the East.

Still more different from the English is the inner man ; naturally mirthful and expansive, witty, careless, even giddy, quarrelsome from mere love of noise, prompt to enthusiasm or despondency, imbued with the love of literary form and legal subtleties, he is the Frenchman of the West, as the Pole or the Japanese are Frenchmen of the East. And always there has been an affinity of nature, a harmony of thought, between them and us. At once we feel we are cousins. Their ancestors formerly came in thousands to fight under our flag. Our revolutions were always felt in Ireland. So strong, for nations as well as individuals, is that mysterious tie of a common origin, or even the most remote consanguinity.

Does this mean that the Irishman, thanks to his insular position, has escaped all cross breeding and remained pure Celt ? Far from it. No country was oftener or more cruelly invaded than his. The stranger implanted himself in it, begat his children there, introduced in the race elements that are still recognizable ; for example, that most peculiar expression of the eyes, the height of the cheek-bones, the outline of the temples and cranium, which are in many cases clearly Scandinavian.

In the origin of history the primitive inhabitants of Erin, the Firbolgs (men with the skin of beasts) were vanquished by the Thuathan-de-Danan, "the fairy people," who came from the East, and who founded the realm of Innisfallen, or Island of Fate. A Spanish invasion (probably Phenician), that of the Milesians, overthrew that establishment ten or twelve centuries before the Christian era, and three hundred years before the foundation of Rome. After that came an uninterrupted list of one hundred and ninety-seven Milesian kings, who reached to the arrival of the Northmen, in the eighth century of the present era. Under their rule Ireland enjoyed a profound peace. It was during this period of more than a thousand years that flourished and developed in the island of Erin an entirely original civilization, characterised by the Brehon Code, by customs of great gentleness, by institutions of admirable prudence, among others that of a national militia, the *Fiana-Erin*, or *Fenians*, who were recruited by voluntary enlistment, defended the country and maintained order therein, while the citizens pursued their various avocations,—agriculture, in which they excelled, fishing and navigation, for which they displayed some ability.

Divided into five or six small independent kingdoms Ireland, without her militia, would have fallen an easy prey to the Britons, the Gauls, or the Caledonians, and later on to the Romans. Thanks to that national force,—a true civic guard, quartered during winter on the inhabitants, and ever popular, which proves that it knew how to preserve intact the tradition of Celtic virtues,—Ireland, alone almost among European nations, escaped a Roman invasion. After twelve hundred years the remembrance of the Fenians has remained so vivid in the hearts of the people that the Irish Republicans of America, when they resumed in our own days the struggle in arms against England, naturally chose the name of the ancient defenders of national independence.

With the fall of the Roman Empire and the dying out of the fear of invasion, the Fenian institution disappeared. The military instincts of the nation then manifested themselves at the exterior by frequent incursions made by Irish adventurers in England, Scotland, or Gaul. It was in one of those incursions off the coast of Brittany that Niall Mor, King of Tara, took prisoner, with several other young Christians, a boy named Sucoth, and whom they called *Patricius* (Patrick) on account of his noble origin. This was at the end of the fourth century of our era. The prisoner was employed in tending flocks in Ireland, spent seven years there, and at last found an opportunity of escaping to his own country. When back in Brittany, he constantly thought with grief of the dreadful destiny of the Irish, who still remained in ignorance of the true religion, and vegetated in the darkness of Druidism. One night he had a prophetic dream, after which he resolved to dedicate himself to the evangelization of those unhappy heathens. To this effect he went to the town of Tours, where he assumed the religious habit, then on to Rome, where he entered the missionary seminary. In the year 432 he was at the Barefooted Augustines' Convent, in Auxerre, when he heard of the death of Paladius, fifth apostolic missionary of the Holy See in the island of Erin. Patrick solicited and obtained the honour of succeeding him. He was made Archbishop *in partibus infidelium*, and set out with twenty other French priests.

A certain number of Christians were already to be found in Ireland; but the bulk of the nation remained attached to its traditional worship, which was that of Chaldea and of Ancient Gaul, the

The Race.

worship of the sun or fire, as the principle of all life and purity.

Yet the sons of Erin were not by any means barbarians; their civilization could rather be regarded as the most flourishing in Europe. They knew the art of weaving stuffs, and of working metals; their laws were wise and just, their customs hardy without ferocity. Patrick knew better than any one that he must think neither of hurrying their conversion nor of imposing it by force. He devoted himself with great adroitness to the task of winning the favour of the chiefs, tenderly handled all the national prejudices, loudly extolled the excellence of the Brehon Code, and succeeded at last in giving baptism to the Princes of Leinster. After this the new religion made such rapid progress that at the end of fifteen years Patrick was obliged to ask for thirty new Bishops from Rome, besides the numerous native priests who had already received ordination at his hands. When he died at the ripe age of one hundred and twenty years, Ireland had become Christian, and was rapidly being Latinised in the innumerable schools attached to the monasteries and churches. She even entered so eagerly in the new path as to deserve the name of "Isle of Saints" throughout the Roman world, and that for a long time it was enough to be Irish or to have visited Erin to become invested with almost a halo of sanctity.

That transformation had been accomplished without violence or effusion of blood. Until the 8th century it was a source of honour and prosperity for Ireland, for the lustre of her own civilization was enhanced by her renown for piety, and all the neighbouring nations sent their sons in flocks to be instructed in her arts and her virtues.

But the very virtues that made her a country of monks and scholars were doomed before long to become the source of all her misfortunes. When the Scandinavian invasions began to pour over the whole of Europe, Ireland, emasculated by an entirely mystical devotion, was found incapable of sustaining the shock of the Northmen. The disappearance of the Fenian Militia had for a long time left her without a national tie, given up to local rivalries, and broken in pieces, as it were, by the clan system. At the very time that she most urgently needed a powerful central authority to struggle against the *black* and *white strangers* from Norway and Denmark, she was found defenceless, and it was not her feeble belt of mountains, opening everywhere on deep bays, that could oppose a serious barrier to them, or guard her plains against their invasions.

Pressed by hunger, the Scandinavians left their country in shoals. They threw themselves on the coasts of Great Britain, France, and Spain, as far as the basin of the Mediterranean. In no place were the people of Europe, already enfeebled by habits of comparative luxury, able to resist those giants of the North, who dauntlessly embarked in their otter-skin boats and dared to go up the Seine even to the very walls of Paris. Ireland was a prey marked out for them. If peradventure the invading party were not numerous enough and were beaten back by numbers, they would come back in thousands the following year and sweep all before them. Vainly did the sons of Erin fight with all the courage of despair; one after the other their chieftains were vanquished, and the foe definitely took up a position on the south-east coast, where he founded the cities of Strangford, Carlingford, and Wexford.

Not content with reducing the Irish to bondage, the victors took a cunning and savage delight in humiliating and degrading them, lodging garnisaries under their roofs, interdicting, under pain of death, the exercise of all liberal arts as well as the carrying of arms, destroying schools, burning books to take possession of the gold boxes that protected their precious binding.

Every ten or twelve years a liberator sprang up in the West or North, and tried to shake off the abhorred yoke. But the rebellion only made it weigh more heavily on the neck of the vanquished; and if it happened that a Brian Boru succeeded, after incredible efforts and heroism, in gathering troops numerous enough to inflict on the stranger a bloody defeat, such a day of glory was invariably followed by the most sinister morrow.

After two centuries of slavery, interrupted by massacres, vain struggles, and impotent efforts, Ireland, once so prosperous, gradually sank in the darkest state of barbarism. The intestine dissensions and the rivalries between clans achieved the work of the Northern Conquerors. In the year 1172 she was ripe for new masters, also of Scandinavian race, who were ready to swoop on her with their Anglo-Saxon bands, after passing, to come to her, through the duchy of Normandy and through Great Britain.

Henry the Second of Anjou, King of England, was resolved to add Ireland to his possessions. All he wanted was a pretext. He found it in the state of practical schism and independence into which the insular Church had fallen. The members of its clergy no longer recognized the Roman discipline, did not observe Lent, and married like those of the Greek rite. Henry the Second solicited and obtained from Pope Adrian II. a bull authorizing him to invade the sister isle, in order to "re-establish therein the rule of the Holy See, stop the progress of vice, bring back respect for law and religion, and secure the payment of St. Peter's pence." But in spite of this formal authorization he was too much occupied with Aquitaine to be able to entertain seriously the idea of undertaking the conquest of Ireland, when one of his vassals, Strongbow, cut the knot by landing on the island at the head of a Welsh army, to carve himself a kingdom on the south-east coast.

The way was open; Henry II. threw himself in it in his turn, and established himself in the east of the island, where, strong in the countenance of the clergy secured to him by the Papal bull, he received before long the homage of the principal native chieftains.

Limited at first to a territory enclosed within palisades, or *Pale*, which, during more than four centuries, enlarged or got narrowed, according to the fortune of war and the relative strength of the belligerent parties, the English rule was destined at last to spread over the whole of the island. But, of this seven-century struggle, the last word is not yet said. The wound is ever bleeding. Ireland has never accepted her defeat; she refuses to accept as valid a marriage consummated by a rape. Always she protested, either by direct rebellion, when she found the opportunity for it, as in 1640, in 1798, and in 1848; either by the voice of her poets and orators, by the nocturnal raids of her *Whiteboys* and *Ribbonmen*, by the plots of her Fenians, by the votes of her electors, by parliamentary obstruction, by passive resistance, by political or commercial interdict—opposed to the intruder; in a word, by all the means, legal or illegal, that offered to interrupt prescription.

A striking, and, one may say, a unique example in history: after seven centuries of sustained effort on the part of the victor to achieve his conquest, this conquest is less advanced than on the morrow of Henry the Second's landing at Waterford. An abyss still severs the two races, and time, instead of filling up that abyss, only seems to widen it. This phenomenon is of such exceptional and tragic interest; it beats with such crude light on the special physiology of two races and the general physiology of humanity, that one needs must stop first and try to unravel its tangible causes if one be desirous of comprehending what is taking place in the land of Erin.

CHAPTER VI.

HISTORICAL GRIEVANCES.

The English, it must be admitted, are no amiable masters. Never, in any quarter of the globe, were they able to command the goodwill of the nations submitted to their rule, nor did they fascinate them by those brilliant qualities that often go a long way towards forgiveness of possible injuries. "Take yourself off there, that I may take your place," seems always to have been the last word of their policy. Pure and simple extermination of autochthon races; such is their surest way to supremacy. One has seen it successively in America, on the Australian continent, in Tasmania, in New Zealand, where the native tribes hardly exist now more than as a memory. On the other hand, if the vanquished races were too numerous or too sturdy and prolific to be easily suppressed, as in India or Ireland, reconciliation never took place; conquest ever remained a doubtful and precarious fact.

In Ireland, the question was made more complex by two elements that visibly took a predominant part in the relations between the conquerors and the conquered. In the first place, the island of Erin, having remained outside the pale of the Roman world and of barbaric invasions, possessed an indigenous and original civilization that made her peculiarly refractory to the establishment of the feudal system. Secondly, her very remoteness and her insular character inclined the immigrants to establish themselves there regretfully, to consider her always as a colony and a place of exile, where they only resided against their will. For the first four hundred years of their occupation they confined themselves to the eastern coast within the inclosed territory (varying with the fortune of war) that they called the *Pale* or palisade, and outside which the Irish preserved their manners, their laws, and their own customs.

In spite of this barrier, it happened in the course of time that the English colonists got pervaded by those customs and felt their contagion. At once the British Parliament had recourse to drastic laws in order to open a new abyss between the two races, and keep the mastery they had over the Irish. Such is the special object of an edict of Edward III., known under the name of *Edict of Kilkenny*, and by which it is reputed high treason for any Englishman established in Ireland to have married an Irishwoman, to have legitimised an Irish child, or have held him in baptism, to have taken an Irish Christian name, to have worn the Irish dress, to have spoken the Erse tongue, to have let his moustache grow, or to have ridden saddleless, as was the Irish fashion; above all, to have submitted to the Brehon Code. Those divers crimes were punished by confiscation of property, and perpetual imprisonment of the offender.

Such laws were a powerful obstacle to fusion, raised by the intruder himself. One sees at once the difference between, for instance, such a system and that established by the Norman invasion in Great Britain.

Here the conqueror found a race made supple by Roman occupation and Danish rule; he established himself, by strength of arm, on the soil, covered it with strongholds, and everywhere substituted himself to the dispossessed masters; he at once implanted within his new dominions the French tongue, the feudal system, the powerful hierarchy that constituted its strength; he remained standing, iron-covered and in arms, over the prostrate bodies of the population in bondage, and repressed with such a high hand any attempt at rebellion, that the very idea of resistance must of necessity die out soon. On the other hand, having transplanted himself, and without any idea of return, in this new sphere, he immediately submitted to its influence; he incorporated himself with the ambient race to such a degree as soon to forget his own origin, and come after two or three generations to consider himself as purely of English breed.

In Ireland, on the contrary, not only was the conqueror reduced by the imperfect state of his conquest to remain on the defensive, confined within the Pale on the eastern shore, within reach, so to say, of the mother country; not only could not he dream for a long time of obliging populations that escaped all action on his part to obey his manners and his laws; not only did he systematically keep those populations at arm's length and avoided mixing with them; but periodical laws and edicts constantly came to remind them, on pain of terrible punishment, that he belonged to another race, and must guard with jealous care the integrity of its autonomy. Without any intercourse with the more distant tribes, he was at constant war with those of the borders of the Pale.

And war was, at this period even still more than in

our own days, mere rapine, raised to the dignity of a system. The English did not scruple to make incursions on their neighbour's lands, to take away harvest, cattle, and women, after which they returned to their fortified territory.

They did even worse: having heard of the ancient custom by which the Irish formerly accorded fire and candle light to their national militia or Fenians, the English revived it to their own profit; they quartered on the peasantry in their neighbourhood during all the winter, a soldier, who took his seat round the domestic hearth, shared the meals of the family, took possession of the best bed—nay, did not disdain to cast the eye of favour on the wife or daughter—and not the less remained a stranger, a foe, at the same time that he was a forced guest and a spy—for he was forbidden to speak the language, to adopt the dress, to imitate the manners of his victims. . . . The horror of that burden coming anew every year had once led to the suppression of the Fenian militia. How much more terrible was such servitude, enforced by the enemy! Constant were the rebellions, and always repressed with calculated barbarity—they only served as a pretext for new exactions.

Historical Grievances.

Still, in spite of all, a certain contagion of habits took place between the contiguous races. A few native chiefs insensibly began to imitate the manners of the English. The English were not long in discovering a way to reconcile them—by appealing to their basest impulses.

Until then, the Irish had had no knowledge of individual property. With them land was, like the sky or the air they breathed, the common inheritance of those who occupied it. The members of a clan, indeed, paid the chieftain a tax or annual duty, but they did not conceive it as possible that this leader could look on himself as the master of the social fund to which they, like him, had a hereditary right. At the most they expected their harvest or cattle to be seized, in case of non-payment of the tax. There never had been an eviction of the tenant, as there had been no sale or transfer of the land by him occupied. Individual appropriation, as resulting from the feudal system, was such a new idea to the Irish that they were at first unable to grasp it.

"What interest can you have in making your clan give up their land to the English, since you get it back in return for your homage?" would ask some of the native chieftains of those of their countrymen nearer the pale who had taken for some time to performing that commercial transaction.

The neophytes of feudal law would then explain that in case of extension of the English conquest, their possession of the land would be guaranteed by the fact of the new title. What they took great care should not be discovered by the clan, was that they gave what did not belong to them, and sold the collective property of their followers, to receive it afterwards at the hands of the English as personal property . . . . This was seen clearly later on, when they began to sell it or raise mortgages on it. But that, the dawn of a gigantic fraud, nobody in Ireland could so much as suspect. The fraudulent origin of individual appropriation is nevertheless, even to our own day, the true root of the desperate resistance that the Irish tenant invariably opposes to eviction. Be it tradition, be it "cellular memory," he is conscious of his primordial and superior right to that glebe once stolen from his forefathers.

Stolen! if only it had been stolen once for all! . . . . . But to repeat Fitzgibbon's (Lord Clare) saying, there is not in the whole of Ireland one field that has not been *at least three times* unjustly taken from its legitimate possessors. And that spoliation was always accompanied by the most aggravating circumstances.

It was indeed with Henry VIII. and Elizabeth that the true efforts of England to achieve the conquest of Erin were made, and from that time, to the antagonism of the two races, to the conflict of interests, was added religious hatred. Between puritanical England and Catholic Ireland began a duel to the death, into which each generation in turn has thrown itself for three centuries. Oppression begets rebellion, and rebellion expires drowned in blood. We have no intention of repeating that history in these pages; its details are to be found everywhere. Let us only recall its essential features.

Towards the year 1565, Queen Elizabeth undertook the "plantation" of Ireland on a large scale, and set about it by the elementary process of dispossessing the owners of the soil in order to present Englishmen with their lands. The whole country rose, under the command of John Desmond, who called the Spaniards to his aid. Upon which England sent to Ireland, together with Sydney, Sussex, and Walter Raleigh, armies whose instructions were "the extermination of the Rebels."

"At Christmas," wrote one of the English Generals,

Sir Nicolas Malby, in the year 1576, "I entered Connaught, and soon finding that by mercy I should only succeed in having my throat cut, I preferred to adopt a different tactic. I therefore threw myself in the mountains with the settled determination of destroying these people by sword and fire, sparing neither the old nor the children. *I burnt down all their harvests and all their houses, and I put to the sword all that fell within my hands* . . . . This occurred in the country of Shane Burke. I did the same thing in that of Ullick Burke."

The other English Generals vied in ardour with this butcher; so much so that at the end of a few years of indiscriminate hangings, massacres, burnings of house and land, the whole of Munster was laid waste like a desert; a few wretches only were left to wander over it like ghosts, and they came voluntarily to offer their throat to the knife of Queen Elizabeth's soldiers. The Virgin Queen then resolved to repeople that desert; she made proclamation that all the lands of the Desmonds were confiscated (more than 500,000 acres) and she offered them gratuitously to whosoever would "plant" them with the help of English labour. The grantees were to pay no duty to the Crown until six years had passed, and that duty was always to be of the lightest. In spite of these advantages colonization did not make much progress. The English at last understood that they must either give it up, or resign themselves to having the ground cultivated by the despoiled Irish who had survived the massacres. How could those wretched people have done otherwise than nourish the hope of revenge?

That revenge was attempted in Ulster at the death of Elizabeth. It ended in new disasters, new tortures, new confiscations. The counties of Tyrone, Derry, Donegal, Armagh, Fermanagh, and Cavan,—in all about three million acres,—were then seized by the Crown and distributed in lots to Scotch settlers.

In the year 1641, under the reign of Charles I., a few Irishmen having emigrated to the continent, and having been initiated to modern military tactics in the ranks of the French army, attempted to liberate their country. They provoked a rising, succeeded in holding in check during eight years all the British forces, and in 1649 compelled the King of England to grant them by formal treaty the conditions they themselves dictated. But a few days later the head of Charles fell on the scaffold, and Cromwell in person, escorted by his son, by Ireton and Ludlow, made it his business to come and annul the treaty of Kilkenny.

"For Jesus! . . . No quarter! . . ." Such was the battle-cry he gave to his Roundheads. Drogheda, then Wexford were taken by storm; men, women, and children were exterminated; Galway fell in 1652. The populations, exhausted by a war and famine of ten years' duration, surrendered themselves to his mercy, and laid down their arms. Cromwell had only now to reap the fruits of his victory by making Ireland pay for it.

His first idea was to complete the extermination of the native race, in order to replace it by English colonists. But even his gloomy soul recoiled before the only means that at once and for ever could put an end to "the Irish gangrene." He adopted a middle course, of much less radical efficacy. This middle course consisted in transporting, or, as they called it at the time *transplanting* all the Irish into the region bounded by the Shannon, there to be penned up like men infested with the plague, while all the rest of the territory was allotted to English families.

The enterprise was conducted with truly puritanical method and rigour. Thousands of Irish were shipped as slaves to the West Indies, thousands of others were imprisoned in Connaught, under pain of death for whoever should cross its limits. All the land, carefully parcelled out, was divided by lot between the soldiers of Cromwell, upon agreement that they should consider themselves bound to expend their pay for three years on the improvement of it. But those fields, to yield up their value, had to be cultivated, and the English labourer declined to become a voluntary exile in order to cultivate them. Little by little the native peasantry came back to their old homes with the tenacity peculiar to their class, they founded families and reconstituted the Irish nation under the ten or twelve thousand landlords imposed over them by fraud and violence. Forty years after Cromwell's death, these landlords had even forgotten how to speak the English language.

Restoration was not destined to heal any of those cruel wounds. Charles II. took little heed of Ireland, which he deemed too far off, and besides he thought it good policy not to disturb the new occupants in their possessions. He barely deemed it necessary to establish in Dublin a Court of Revision that sat only one year, examined no more than seven hundred cases out of a total of above three thousand that were submitted to it, and ordered the restitution of hardly a sixth part of the confiscated land.

After the Revolution of 1688, nevertheless, the Irish only embraced with more ardour the cause of James II. when he landed in Ireland with a handful of men. Even after his defeat at the Boyne, they so successfully resisted William of Orange that he was compelled in 1691 to grant to them, by the treaty of Limerick, the free exercise of their religion and the political privileges that could help them to preserve it. But, like so many other charters, that one was soon to be violated. All the Irish Jacobites were compelled to expatriate themselves (numbers of them took service in France; more than fifty thousand Irishmen died under the *fleur-de-lis* during the first half of the eighteenth century); four thousand others were evicted from one million of acres that William distributed among his followers. Soon to this already terrible repression were to be added all the rigours of the Penal Code, that code that proclaimed it a duty to spy, and a meritorious act to betray the Irishman at his hearth; that code of which Burke could say: "Never did the ingenious perversity of man put forth a machine more perfect, more thoughtfully elaborated, more calculated to oppress, to impoverish, to degrade a people, to lower in them human nature itself."

Under the network of that nameless despotism which attacked man in his dearest privileges, the rights of conscience, the sanctity of home,—under the weight of a legislation that in a manner forbade her the use of water and fire, that closed all careers before her, after having wrenched her last furrow from her keeping,—the Irish nation persisted in living and multiplying. Was it any wonder that in the depth of her collective soul she cherished dreams of revenge and justice?

The American Emancipation and the French Revolution appeared to her as the dawn of regeneration. Alas! once again the glorious effort of 1798,—the rebellion in arms, victory itself, were only to end in a complete wreck. As if Fate owed one more stroke of irony to this martyred nation, it was an Irish Parliament that by its own vote in 1800 abdicated the hardly recovered national independence. Pitt bought it wholesale for the price of 1,200,000 guineas.

It was not enough, however, to have taken from the Irishman his blood, his land, his religious faith, and his liberty: they must still prevent his prospering in commerce or industry. Political interest was here in accordance with avarice in giving this advice to the victor.

Charles II. began by forbidding Ireland to export meat, butter, and cheese to England. At that time of slow maritime intercourse, no idea could be entertained of sending them to any other market. The Irish had to fall back on wool, which they exported to France and Spain. That was sufficient to arouse the jealousy of their pitiless masters. The export of wool, be it as raw material or in woven stuffs, was forbidden the Irish on pain of confiscation and fines.

The effect of this harsh measure was two-fold: it prevented the abhorred Irish prospering; it secured to the English merchant the monopoly of Irish wool, which he could henceforth buy at his own price (generally at a quarter of the current price), and sell again at a lesser rate than all his competitors. It only remained for Ireland to make smugglers of all her fishermen; they crammed all the caverns on her coasts with wool, and during the winter, in spite of excisemen, they exchanged it for the wines and spirits of France and Spain. By the same occasion they exported soldiers and imported Catholic priests. Thus did Ireland keep losing her vital strength, by the constant departure of the most vigorous amongst her sons, at the same time that she inoculated in her blood two equally fatal poisons—alcohol and fanaticism.

On the other hand, the Puritan weavers of Ulster were ruined like the wool-farmers. They emigrated to America, and England found no bitterer foes than their sons during the War of Independence.

Some of the Irish tried to fall back on other industries, as the weaving of linen or ship-building. At once England interfered with an iron hand by establishing the most ruinous prohibitive duties on Irish linens, while at the same time her cotton fabrics came pouring over the country. To make doubly sure, England, by a special law, formally interdicted ship-building in Ireland as well as any direct trade with any foreign market whatsoever.

One feels a sort of shame for the human kind in having to record such consistent acts of systematic cruelty. The violence of military retaliation, the sacking of towns or the massacre of vanquished foes, may be explained by the heat of combat, and are found in the annals of all countries. An economical compression exercised during ten or twelve generations on one nation by another nation of Shylocks is, happily, a fact without any parallel in history.

From the beginning of the 18th century all industrial enterprise had thus been unmercifully forbidden to Ireland. All the factories were closed, the working population had been reduced to field labour, emigration or street-begging. This population therefore weighed still more heavily on the soil, still exaggerating its tendencies to subdivision; which tendencies, already a curse for Ireland, were to cause in the future new ferments of hatred and misery. All the attempts that Ireland made to free herself from those iron shackles were pitilessly repressed. She saw herself deprived of her right to commercial activity, as she had been of national conscience, of land, and religious or political freedom. And it is after having thus for centuries systematically trained the Irish to poverty, idleness, and drink, that England, crowning her work with calumny, dares to bring forward their vices as an excuse for herself!

These things are far from us already. But it would be erring greatly to imagine that in the eyes of the Irish they bear an antiquated character. Oral tradition, seconded by an indigenous literature, keeps the wound open and green. Yonder wretched beggar, dying of hunger and want upon the glebe once possessed by his ancestors, knows that they ruled where he now serves, bears their name with a touching pride, and sadly toils for others in a field that he believes to belong to himself. He is not ignorant of the way in which it was taken from him, at what date, and in what manner the event took place. How could he consider its present possessors otherwise than as his most cruel enemies?

Let us imagine the French *émigrés* brought back violently on the lands taken from them by the nation, and reduced to support their family by tilling their fields with their own hands. Let us suppose them compelled every year to pay an exorbitant rent to the usurper. Let us blot out from history's page the milliard indemnity given to the *émigrés* and the amnesty passed over those things by five or six successive revolutions. Let us lastly add to these deadly rancours the weight of a religious persecution of three centuries, of the undisguised contempt of the victor, and of the most shocking political inequality. . . . Let that *émigré*, in a word, not only have lost caste, be spoliated and a serf, but also be a pariah, a kind of pestilent member of the community: then we shall gather some idea of the state of mind of the Irish people towards England; we shall understand that in truth the only mistake committed by Cromwell and the others in their system of colonization was to have not carried it to its full length, to have not exterminated all by fire or sword, and to have left a single son of Erin alive.

As a contrast to England and Ireland, let us place a historical fact of the same order, that of France with Corsica. Here also we find an insular race of markedly distinct character, of different language, different manners and traditions, the habit of independence and the clan-spirit,—all that can foster and serve resistance to annexation. But here the conquering nation is France, and she is a kind mother. She does not come, fire and sword in hand, to ravage the harvests of the vanquished, to take his land, to impose on him, together with a new faith, exceptional laws, and a brand of infamy. On the contrary, to them she opens her arms, she offers her wealth and her love. From the first day she admits Corsicans to the provincial parliaments, and twenty years later she receives their deputies in the Assemblée Nationale. From the first hour they feel they are Frenchmen, the equals of those born in the Ile de France. There are for them neither special taxes, nor political inferiority, nor rigours of any sort. Never was an inch of ground taken from them to be given to the continental families. Never were they treated like serfs to be trodden down without mercy. If there be an exception made, it is in their favour; as, for instance, the reduction of one half of all duties on imports; the free trade in tobacco; the enormous proportion of Corsicans admitted to all Government offices.

But what a difference, too, in the results! . . . In less than a hundred years, the fusion between the two races is so perfect, the assimilation so complete, that one could not find to-day one man in Corsica to wish for a separation. Nay, rather, against such an enterprise, if any one were found to attempt it, all Corsica would rise in arms.

If Great Britain had so willed it, Ireland might easily have become to her what Corsica is to us. Only, for the last seven hundred years, Great Britain has lacked what alone could have made that miracle possible,—a mother's heart and love.

CHAPTER VII.

KILLARNEY.

I know no place to compare with Killarney: so soft to the eye, so full of unspeakable grace. It is as a compendium of Ireland; all the characteristic features of the country are united there: the elegant "round towers," drawing on the horizon the airy outline of their conic shafts; the soft moistness of the atmosphere, the tender blue of the sky, the intense green of the meadows, set off by long, black trails of peat, and the white, ochre, and red streaks which the grit-stone and clay-slate draw on the hill-side.

Within the oval circus formed by the mountains of Kerry, the Killarney lakes succeed one another like small Mediterraneans, all dotted with lovely islands, where myrtle and rare ferns grow freely, fostered by a Lusitanian climate. Every one of those islands has its legend, its own saint, buried under some old moss-grown mound; its ruined castle, its ivy-clothed abbey, paved with tombstones and haunted by some *banshee.* They are like large baskets of flowers floating on the clear, silent waters, whose peace is only broken now and then by the jumping of a fish, or the clucking of some stray teal. All there unite to form a landscape of almost paradoxical beauty. You think you have landed in fairyland, outside the pale of ordinary life.

The most illustrious of them is Innisfallen, where the monks wrote in the seventh century their famous *Annals*, the pride of the Bodleian Library. In viewing this enchanting island, you involuntarily fall to repeating the beautiful lines of Moore which you used to bungle in your school days, and of which you first realise the profound truth:

> "*Sweet Innisfallen, fare thee well,*
> *May calm and sunshine long be thin ,*
> *How fair thou art, let others tell,*
> *While but to feel how fair be mine, etc.*"

Along the shores of that range of lakes, two lordly domains display the noble arrangement of their parks: one is the seat of the Earl of Kenmare, lord-lieutenant of the county, late Lord Chamberlain to the Queen during the Gladstone Ministry. The other belongs to Captain Herbert of Muckross, late Member of Parliament. As far around as you can see the land belongs to either of those two landlords. Just as in the tale, down to the extremity of the valley, up to the very top of the far-away mountain, land and water, beasts and Christians, all belong to the "Marquis de Carabas."

Some restriction must be made, however. Changes have been introduced lately. Only a few years ago it was a thing understood that of the two members which the borough returned to Parliament one must be the heir presumptive of the house of Kenmare, the other the chief of the house of Muckross. That is over. Now-a-days the Kerry voters send whom Mr. Parnell likes to the House of Commons. But the air of the parks is still the property of the two owners; none may breathe it without their leave. I hasten to say that the permission is most courteously given by Lord Kenmare to all tourists, and as readily (if less liberally) sold on the Muckross grounds to anyone willing to pay one or two shillings, according to his approach walking or on horseback.

The two parks are marvels, almost without other rivals in the world, for their prodigious extent, their admirably kept shrubberies and avenues, and the splendour and variety of the points of view which art has devised on the lakes. Those lakes themselves, with their islands, bays, and toy-peninsulas, their rippling brooks and foaming cascades, are only part of the beauties of the whole. Muckross is proud to possess the old abbey of the same name, and the Torc Cascade. Kenmare boasts Innisfallen, Ross Island, Saint Finian's Tomb, the legendary ruins of O'Donoghue's Castle, and a hundred other wonders. It is more regal than lordly, and there are indeed few royal residences which can boast such gardens.

You go away dazzled, enchanted, intoxicated with verdure, ozone, and poetic sights. You come back the day following, you almost wish to take root there for a sort of contemplative life, where you would discard any heavier occupation than catching salmon, smoking endless cigarettes, and reading over your favourite authors. A rich artist, it is said, being pricked with a violent desire of that kind, offered I don't know how much ready money to Lord Kenmare if he would grant him five hundred square yards of ground on Ross Island. The offer was declined.

There is a reverse side to the picture; and it could scarcely be less brilliant. Killarney is a sorry borough of about four or five thousand inhabitants, more miserable looking than words can express. Except in the great hotels which English enterprise has raised for fleecing the tourists attracted there by the beauty of the lakes, there is not a vestige of ease or prosperity. No busy workman, not one manufacture is to be seen. The miserable shops exhibit a few dusty wares which nobody seems anxious either to buy or to sell. There is a despondent stillness about, and people look tired with doing nothing. The women, all more or less "tattered and torn," wear a poor rag of a shawl on their heads. Half-naked children, wild-haired, full of vermin, swarm out of all the small alleys which open on the one street of the town. Only the Anglican and Catholic churches rise above the sordid little dwellings with a substantial and well-to-do air.

Go out of the village, follow the long walls which enclose the lordly seats, and after three or four miles you will find again the Irish country such as you have seen it everywhere. Turnip and barley fields, thin pastures, few trees or none at all. On the road-side occasionally is a consumptive cow, or a pig wallowing in mud fraternally with two or three bright-eyed urchins. Here and there a hovel with the traditional dung-hill and three hens. Nothing, in short, calculated to bring a new light on the agrarian crisis.

It is in Kerry, however, that the malady has reached its most acute state, they all tell me. But you could not believe how hard it is to obtain any definite information about those matters. People who really know about it feel a sort of shame to bare their national wounds before a stranger, and besides, the diversity of judgments makes it difficult to draw something positive from them. Every man has his party feeling, and is wishing to enforce it upon you. Provided with a good number of letters of introduction, and everywhere received with perfect cordiality, I have talked already with people of all conditions — landlords, agents, farmers, doctors, priests, and labourers,—without having obtained as yet any but individual views. Home Rulers and Orangemen have made me hear arguments that I know by heart from having heard them repeated these last eight years, ever since the crisis entered its actual phase. This is not the thing we want : we want *espèces*, as they say in French law ; specific illustration, direct symptoms of the Irish disease.

And that is the difficulty. The habit of living among certain deformities so familiarises us with them that we are no longer able to perceive them, and still less to point them out. Moreover, when upon receiving a letter from London, a man is kind enough to ask you to dinner, to introduce you to his wife and daughters, to lend you his horse and trap, and to empty for your benefit his store of ready-made opinions, is it possible decently to ask him more? He has his own affairs, and cannot spend his time running with you through hill and dale in order to help you to unravel a sociological problem.

By a stroke of good luck I met the scout I wanted.

I was returning from an excursion to the Gap of Dunloe when, on the banks of the river which waters the Kenmare estate, near the bridge, I noticed a man of about forty, of middle height, poorly but neatly clad, who was walking in front of me and gave evident signs of wishing to enter into conversation. I had been so harassed lately by the swarm of cicerones and incompetent guides who crowd all ways to the lakes and sights around Killarney, that I had grown suspicious, and pretended not to see the man. But he had his idea and stuck to it. Slackening his pace, he began to whistle *La Marseillaise*.

That was saying plainly:—

"You are French, and I am a friend of France like all Irishmen. You are welcome here."

Throughout the world it is the adopted form for such a declaration of love. On board a transatlantic steamer or in the sitting-rooms of a cosmopolite hotel, when a fair-haired or dark-haired new acquaintance seats herself to the piano and begins to play the march of Rouget de l'Isle, the French tourist can see his way: he is looked upon with no unfriendly eye.

There were no dark or fair tresses here, but only a bearded pepper-and-salt quadragenarian, with the patent purpose of hooking me at the rate of half-a-crown an hour: so I remained obdurate. But he, suddenly making up his mind:—

"Well, *Sor*," he said to me with a soft voice and the most enticing smile, "how do you *loike* our country?"

"Your country? I should like it a great deal better if one could go about it without being pestered by guides at every turning," I said, but half-remorsefully.

"How true, sir! Those guides positively infest the place. And if they only knew their trade! But they are regular swindlers, beggars who steal the tourist's money; the shame of Ireland, that is what they are!"

The conversation then commenced, and to say the truth I have no reason to repent it. The fellow is well-informed, quick-witted, incredibly talkative, and in five minutes has given me really valuable information, besides biographical details about himself. He is called MacMahon like many others in this country, for I have seen that name over twenty village shops already. Is he any relation to the Maréchal? No; he makes no pretension to that. But after all it is not improbable that they come from one root, for my friend is not, of course, without his relationship with some of the numberless kings of Ireland.

"And the Marshal is a great man, a brave soldier, a true Irishman. I have his picture at home. I'll show it to you if you do me the honour to visit my humble roof, and accept a glass of 'mountain dew.'"

My new acquaintance has been quill-driver at a land surveyor's, and he knows many things. This, for instance: that all people here, from the most insignificant farmer to the biggest landowner, are in debt.

"All that glitters is not gold," he says, with a melancholy smile. "Do you see that large expanse of land, sir? Well, those who own it are not perhaps richer than I, and have not perhaps always as much pocket-money as would be convenient for them. Their annual income goes to pay the interest of an enormous debt, the hereditary obligations which weigh on the property, and the normal keeping of it. Mr. Herbert, the owner of Muckross, had to emigrate to America, where he is now an attorney's clerk, for his daily bread. The shilling you give for entering his park goes to the scraping of it. As for Lord Kenmare, he never sees as much as the tenth part of the revenue of his property, let alone his being forbidden his own grounds under pain of being shot dead! Lady Kenmare lives there alone with her children under protection of a detachment of the police." So the masters of those two noble estates are exiled from them, one by mortgage, the other by agrarian hatred. O, irony of things!

"But Lord Kenmare's not a bad landlord, is he?" I said to MacMahon.

"Far from it. His tenants are eight hundred in number, and there are not three evicted in the year. I know personally twenty of them who owe him four years' rent and are never troubled about it. But he has taken position against the League—that is enough. And then, don't you know, sir, the best of landlords is not worth much in the eyes of his tenants. *They want the land and they will have it.* But this is my house. Please come in, sir."

Thus chattering, the communicative Celt had brought me to the entrance of a small low house in a by-street of Killarney. We entered a sort of kitchen-parlour on a level with the lane. No carpet or flooring of any kind but the simple beaten clay, a large old-fashioned chimney, a table, a few straw-covered chairs; on the walls a whole private museum in chromo-lithography: Pope Pius IX., the Marshal Duke of Magenta, Mr. Parnell, &c., and a branch of holy palm.

Upon our coming, a poor creature, pale and emaciated, had risen without showing any surprise.

"Mrs. MacMahon, *Sor!* Everilda Matilda, a French gentleman who honours our house by stopping a moment in it. Call the children, my dear; the gentleman will be pleased to see them, I think."

A tall girl with brown eyes first presents herself, then a boy between twelve and thirteen years old, then a variety of younger fry. I am told that Mary has passed successfully her "standards," that Tim has just begun Latin with an ultimate view to become a priest "like his uncle Jack;" then the "mountain dew" is produced. It is a kind of home-made whisky, not unpalatable.

At last mine host turns to his wife.

"Supposing, my dear, you show your lace to the French gentleman, to let him see what you can do when you are not bed-ridden. Perhaps he will like to bring back some little remembrance of Killarney to his 'lady.'"

I was caught.

Everilda Matilda instantly produced a box containing cuffs and collars of Irish point, and all that remains to me to do, if I am not ready to forfeit my rights to the qualification of gentleman, is to buy a few guineas' worth. Hardly is the matter over, than MacMahon turns to the future ecclesiastic—

"And you, Tim, will you not show the gentleman those sticks you polish so well?"

Caught again!

If each member of the family has his own private trade, the *mountain-dew* threatens to be rather an expensive refreshment.

"I am greatly obliged to you," I said, "but I have got already a complete collection of *shillelaghs*."

MacMahon's jaw fell visibly.

"But we could perhaps make another arrangement, that would be more advantageous," I continued quietly. "You know the country well, you tell me?"

"As a man who has lived forty years in it and never left it."

"Well, let us have a pair of good hacks; you lead me for a couple of days across field and country, and show me a dozen authentic cases of eviction, agrarian violence, or boycottism. If you will undertake this, and I am satisfied with you, upon our return I will take the whole lot of lace."

You should have seen the glowing faces of the whole family! The affair was soon settled, and the day after we started.

CHAPTER VIII.

THROUGH KERRY ON HORSEBACK.

It was not two days but six that we spent, my guide and I, visiting the County Kerry in all directions, examining the crops, asking about prices, entering cottages and small farms, chatting with anyone that we supposed capable of giving us information. The rather unexpected conclusion I arrived at was that the agrarian crisis is more especially felt in the richest districts, while it can hardly be said to exist in the poorest parts. Kerry is, in that particular, a true copy of Ireland on a small scale. It may, in fact, be divided into two perfectly distinct regions—the plains of the north and the mountains of the south-west. Those regions offer characteristics as marked in an economical as in a geographical point of view.

Another conclusion drawn from my personal intercourse with the Irish peasant was that nothing is to be got out of him by bullying and everything by gentle means. If you arrive at an inn and proceed, as do the English everywhere, to assume a harsh and arrogant tone, you will experience the greatest difficulties in obtaining even meagre fare in return for your money. They will pretend they have nothing in the house, that they are not in the habit of receiving travellers, and such like stories. If, on the contrary, you at once proclaim yourself delighted with the country, its manners and its inhabitants; if you risk a compliment to the hostess or a gentle pinch to the children's cheek, the whole house is yours. They will instantly wring the neck of the solitary chicken promenading in front of the house; they will exhibit clean table-linen; they will rush to the neighbour and borrow a salad or some fruit; they will even unearth from some dark corner a bottle of old port. If you give this impromptu supper only half the praise it deserves, you may count on a luxurious breakfast for the next morning. These poor people are thus made. Their heart is warm; their sensibilities are quick. The least thing discourages them; the least thing electrifies them. In contradiction to the Anglo-Saxon serf, who despises his master if he treat him with gentleness, Paddy prefers a gracious word to all the guineas in the kingdom. The philosophical reason for the failure of the British in Ireland (and elsewhere) is perhaps chiefly to be found in their general want of human sympathy. The Englishman speaks too often like a slave-driver when he should speak like an elder brother.

THE PLAIN.

The plains of North Kerry must be classed among the best land in the isle. This is not saying that they are first-class. But they evidently only need some outlay in drainage and manure and a few modern improvements in culture to rival our Normandy pastures. It is above all a land of grazing fields and butter; the grass in the meadows is green and luxuriant; the cows look strong and well. It is evident that the least effort would be sufficient to make agricultural enterprise a thriving business. But carelessness and want of thrift are plainly shown on all sides. Everywhere dung hills, placed just in front of the cottage doors, pour into the ditch the clearest of their virtue. The gardens are ill-kept, the fields transformed into bog for want of a drain seventy feet long. One sees oats so invaded by thistles that it must be a sheer impossibility to get the grain out. In other fields oats rot standing, because no one takes care to cut them in time. Nowhere is any sign shown of vigorous enterprise or activity. Not only do routine and sloth reign all over the country, but one might be tempted to believe in a general conspiracy for wasting the gratuitous gifts of Mother Nature without any profit to anybody.

Yet the country looks relatively rich. The peasantry have good clothes, they despise potatoes, eat bread and meat, drink beer or tea, send their children to school, and appear peculiarly wide awake to their own interests. Are they really, as they declare, unable to pay their rents? That is possible, for the principal products of the country—corn, oats, barley, butter, beef, and mutton, wool and potatoes—have undergone for the last three years a considerable depreciation, estimated at from 15 to 35 per cent. But this depreciation is evidently not felt by a diminution of comfort for the rural populations, here at least. The contrary might even be admitted. In any case there is evidently no question of a crisis of famine such as has so often been seen in this island for the last fifty years. The malady is something else. It is the malady of a people to whom it has been repeated for half a century that the land they live on has been stolen from them by strangers; a people who rightly or wrongly believe this to be the case; a people who have entered, under the direction of a central committee of politicians, on a regular struggle with the landlords; who profit by all economical incidents, especially the fall of prices, if not openly to denounce the treaty, at least to refuse to execute its articles.

A few facts noted in passing will explain the situation better than all discourses.

A large dairy farm, the finest I have yet seen in the country. The buildings are new, the fields covered with thick dark grass. I number sixty-five cows. All the dairy appointments are handsome and well-kept. The farmer looks prosperous. Clearly he lives at ease, judging by the furniture of the house, the quality of his clothes, by the very liberality with which he receives us, and by the brandy which he offers us (he is a friend of my guide). His rent is £100 a year. He does not mean to pay his next term. (*I don't think I will pay this gale.*) His landlord offers to him the sale of his land for a sum of eighteen years' rent, according to the official plan. If he followed that system all he would have to do would be to pay annually during forty-nine years the sum of £78, less by nearly a third than the present farm rent; he would then become a proprietor. He refuses. Why?

"Indeed?" he says, with a wink, "engage myself

for forty-nine years ! . . . *Why ! I shall have the land for nothing in two or three years ! . . .*"

Another well-to-do farmer driving in a dog-cart with his two daughters. The trap is new, the harness smart, the horse strong and well groomed. The damsels wear Dublin hats and white woollen dresses not unfashionable in cut.

"That's what enrages the landlords," my guide says to me; "it is to see tenants come in this style to the Tralee races, cheerfully lose twenty guineas upon a horse, then, when the time for paying the rent arrives, coolly ask for a 40 per cent. reduction on their half-year's rent . . . "

" . . . And in fact it must be enough to make a saint swear ! . . ." he adds philosophically. "But after all, the landlords might be content with the 60 per cent. they get . . . I am sure they get it cheap enough . . . they may think themselves lucky to have even that much, as the interest of confiscated land ! . . . "

That notion of the land being held by its actual detentors through confiscation, may be unfounded in some cases, or even in the majority of cases, but none the less one finds it at the bottom of all Irish syllogisms. And in such cases the real value of the premiss is of little importance; what matters only is the conclusion drawn from it.

A few middling and small farmers.

Maurice Macnamara, Shinnagh: rent, £48 a year; seventeen cows, eight pigs, two horses and one donkey; grass fields, oats, and potatoes; four children, of which one is over twenty years of age. Was able to pay his rent, but was forbidden to do so by the other tenants on the estate, and was in consequence seized by order of the landlord. His neighbours offered to help him to resist the execution. He begged to be left alone, and the moment of the sale having come, he personally bought all his cattle up to the sum due. Nett result of the operation: £11 to pay, over and above the six months' rent. Personal opinion of Maurice Macnamara: it is better to pay £11 than to get a bullet through your head.

John McCarthy, Gwingullier: £16 annual rent, due in May and November; two cows, one horse; oats and potatoes; nine children, the eldest seventeen. Has paid nothing to his landlord since 1883; owes actually £48 to him, and as much to divers tradespeople or usurers. Does not know how he shall get out of it.

Patrick Murphy, Colyherbeer, barony Trughanarkny; was evicted in November from his holding of £28; owed eighteen months' rent. Received from his andlord the offer of being reinstated in the farm on payment of half the sum due, on condition that he would let his crops be sold. Declined the offer, and is perfectly satisfied to receive from the League relief to the amount of £2 a-week. Never saw himself so well off before.

Margaret Callaghan, a widow, close by the town of Kenmare: £8 16s. 4d. rent; one pig, six hens; three small children; four acres of potatoes, three acres waste. Has paid nothing for the last four years. Owes about £20 to various tradespeople. Is not harshly pressed by her landlord, and can practically be considered as owning her bit of ground. Will die of hunger, with her children, the first year the harvest is bad.

Molahiffe, on the road to Tralee.
" This is Mr. Curtin's house."
" And who may Mr. Curtin be ? "

"What! have you never heard of that affair? . . . He was killed last year by the Moonlighters."

"Killed? . . . Was he then a party man, a fierce Orangeman?"

"Mr. Curtin? . . . Not a bit in the world. He was one of the most peaceable, the most Irish at heart, the most esteemed man in this part of the country. His misfortune was to own two rifles. The Moonlighters wanted those weapons. One night they came and demanded them. The ladies of the family were ready to give them up, when Mr. Curtin arrived and looked as if he were going to resist. At once a gun exploded in the passage, and he fell stone dead. . . . That was a warning to everybody. Since that time no one disobeys the moonlighters. But all the same it is unfortunate that the victim should have been Mr. Curtin."

These *Moonlighters* are the direct descendants of the Whiteboys of olden times. They band together and gather at night for the purpose of invading a farm, a solitary house. They are always masked, but sometimes in a very elementary fashion, by pulling down their hat or cap over the face and making two holes through it for the eyes. Normally they ought to search only for arms and to take only arms. But everything degenerates, and the use of force often leads to the abuse of it. The Moonlighters not unfrequently demand a supper, a sum of money, not to speak of the company of some farm-wench to whom they may take a fancy. This impartial offering of violence to house and inmates might lead them far, were they not certain of the discretion of the victims. But the terror they inspire secures impunity to them.

Though everybody in a district knows perfectly well who the intruders are, and though they have often been recognized in spite of the mask, no one dares to reveal their name. They are all too well aware that in case of denunciation a nocturnal bullet will come unerringly to the offender. Besides, a sort of poetical halo and a political mantle of immunity surrounds men who may sometimes, indeed, carry their zeal a little too far, but are after all soldiers in the good cause. The "legitimate" industry of the Moonlighters allows their excesses to be forgotten. A sort of general complicity covers and favours their expeditions.

That complicity goes sometimes to great lengths—for instance the length of non-admitting the intervention of the police in a house where the Moonlighters are performing. The constables perambulating the country hear screams, desperate appeals for help in a farmhouse. They rush to it headlong and knock at the door. At once silence reigns. They are asked from the inside of the house what they want.

"We heard screams. Do you not want protection?"

"What business is that of yours?" is the answer. "Go on your way, and do not come interfering and preventing honest folks enjoying the possession of their house undisturbed!...."

The unlucky constables can only beat a retreat and go their round, often to meet shortly with the Moonlighters, who will laugh at them, having comfortably finished their business.

Before the judges the same thing occurs. Not a witness will give evidence. And if by chance a witness does speak, the jury take care to correct this grave breach of etiquette in their verdict.

The witness, as well as the juryman, has often received a warning. Working alone in the fields, or following a lonely path, he has suddenly seen a little puff of white smoke going up from the bushes some feet in front of him, and he has heard a bullet whizzing over his head. It was a Moonlighter telling him:—

"Be silent, or thou art a dead man."

Castleisland. A small town of little interest,

after the pattern of most Irish boroughs. We stop for lunch at a tavern of rather good appearance, and clearly very popular with the natives. The innkeeper smokes a cigar with us. Is he satisfied with the state of affairs? Yes and no. Certainly he cannot complain—trade in liquor is rather brisk. But there are too many places where one can buy drink in the town—no less than fifty-one.

"And do they all prosper?"

"Nearly all."

"What may their average receipts be?"

"I should say about £400 a year."

£400 multiplied by fifty-one gives £20,400, more than 510,000 francs. And there is not in this place any other industry than agriculture, while statistics I have this moment in my pocket inform me that the aggregate rental of Castleisland is not above £14,000. It is then evident that, times good, times bad, they drink every year here £6,000 worth more in beer and spirits than they would pay in rent to the landlords, if they chose to pay. This seems to be conclusive, as far as Castleisland is concerned. But is there really any reason why the tenants of this district should turn total abstainers for the special purpose of paying the claret and champagne bills of half-a-dozen absentees? Here is the whole problem in a nutshell.

Tralee. The big town of the county, what we should call in France the *chef-lieu*, the seat of the assizes. They are opened precisely at this moment. There are on the rolls three men charged with agrarian murder. I proposed to go and be present at the trials, when I heard that the three cases were to be remanded to the next session, the representative of the Crown having come to the conclusion that the jury would systematically acquit the prisoners, as is so often the case in Ireland.

The Chairman of the Assizes, Mr. Justice O'Brien, seized this occasion to declare, that in the course of an already long career he had never met with a jury having so little regard for their duty. "It must be known widely," he added, "the law becomes powerless when the course of justice is systematically impeded by the very jurymen, as we see it in this country; in which case there is no longer any security for persons or property."

To which the people in Kerry answer that they do not care a bit for English law; what they want is good Irish laws, made in Dublin by an Irish Parliament.

"It is quite true that we have no security here for persons or property," a doctor of the town said to me in the evening. "The outrages were at first exclusively directed against the landlords, rightly or wrongly accused of injustice and harshness in their dealings with their tenants; but for the last two or three years the field of nocturnal aggression has enlarged greatly—a shot now serves to settle any personal quarrel and even trade accounts. In the beginning the jury at least made a distinction between the different motives that actuated the accused. Now they always acquit them, *because they no longer dare to find them guilty*. . . . What will you have? . . . Jurymen are but men. They prefer sending a ruffian at large to paying with their life a too subtle distinction between crimes of an agrarian character and those of another sort. A lump of lead is the most irresistible of arguments. One may assert that presently law has lost all influence in Kerry. It is rapine that reigns, hardly tempered by the decrees of the National League, which of course means only legitimate resistance to the landlords, and by the fund of righteousness possessed at heart by the nation. But let things go on thus only for two years more, we shall have gone back to the savage state."

"Some people tell me, however, that raiding for money is never seen in this part of Ireland."

"Raiding for money never seen! I would rather

say it is the latest development of moonlighting. Any one who covets a piece of his neighbour's land, who wishes to influence his vote for a board of guardians, who is animated by any motive of vulgar greed or spite, has only to set the Moonlighters in motion. The machinery is at hand."

"Could you really give me a few recent instances of moonlighting for money?"

"Of course I could. There is one Daniel Moynihan, at Freemount, near Rathmore: in October, 1886, a party of six men with blackened faces entered his house at night, and breaking open a box, carried away all his money. In January, 1887, at Ballinillane, three men armed with guns entered Daniel Lyne's house and asked for money, threatening to shoot him if he refused; they took away £6. At Faha, in March, 1887, a party of six armed men visited the house of Mr. E. Morrogh Bernard; they demanded money, and got what was in the house."*

"You don't say the League has anything to do with such obvious cases of non-political moonlighting, do you? It is a well-known fact that the

---

* A later instance. On August 30th, 1887, two men armed with guns and wearing masks entered the house of Mr. R. Blennerhasset, at Kells, near Cahirciveen; they went upstairs to Mrs. Blennerhasset's room and demanded money, which they got to the amount of about £5.

organization discountenances moonlighting as well as all other violent practices."

"It does in a manner, but at the same time, by forming in each district a kind of police of the League, an executive body ready for action, it singles out to malignant persons men who may be ready for a private job."

There is obviously considerable exaggeration, or, rather, distortion of facts, in the above statement, as in everything relating to the League on one side or the other. The truth is probably that ruffians, when they want a job in the house-breaking line, ask for nobody's permission, but are only too glad to take moonlighting as a pretence; and thus, common breaches of the law which in ordinary times would go by their proper name, are now ascribed to Moonlighters. The bulk of the population, which is thoroughly honest, has only words of contempt and hatred for what, in justice, should rather be called a deviation than a development of moonlighting.

Nine o'clock at night. In a hollow on the road to Milltown, a man tries to hide himself behind some shrubs; but perceiving that we do not belong to the neighbourhood he shows himself. He is a constable clad in uniform, the black helmet on his head, a loaded gun on his shoulder.

"Why do you seek to avoid attention?"

"Because we are watching that farm-house there on the height, my comrades and I; we have received information to the effect that some men propose to attack it one of these nights; now, we must try not to be seen by the people on the farm, for they would hasten to tell their assailants."

"What! these people would denounce you to those who come to rob them?"

"Just so. We have to protect them against their will. Oh! it is indeed a nice trade to be a constable in Ireland!" &c. &c.

Then follow professional complaints that throw a curious light on the relations between police and population. The unhappy constables are *boycotted* personally and as a body. Nobody speaks to them. It is next to impossible for them to procure the first necessaries of life. Government has to distribute rations to them as to soldiers on a campaign. If they want a conveyance, a cart to transport a detachment of the public force where their presence is wanted, nobody—even among the principal interested—will give means of transport either for gold or silver. The Government have had to give the constabulary special traps that are constantly to be met on the roads, and that one recognizes by their blood-red colour.

That police corps, *the Irish Constabulary Force,* is very numerous, and entails great expense—more than one million and a half sterling per year. The cost would hardly be half a million if the Irish police were on the same footing as the English force; that fact alone can give an adequate idea of the real state of things. Besides, numerous auxiliaries, called *Emergency men,* are always ready to give their help to the regular corps.

Be they soldiers or policemen, Great Britain keeps nearly 50,000 armed men in Ireland. The male adult and able population of the island being under 500,000 men, of whom 200,000 at least are opposed to the agrarian and autonomist movement, one can assume that there is on an average one armed soldier or constable for every six unarmed Irishmen.

On the dusty road before us are slowly walking five cows in rather an emaciated condition. Those beasts strike me by an odd appearance which I am unable to make out at first. When I am close to them I see what it is: *they have no tails.* The absence of that ornament gives the poor animals the awkwardest and most absurd look.

I turn to my guide, who is laughing in his sleeve.

"Look at their master!" he whispers in a low voice.

"Well?"

"The cows have no tails, and the man has no ears. . . ."

It is true. The unlucky wretch vainly endeavoured to hide his head, as round as a cheese, under the brim of his battered old hat; he did not succeed in hiding his deformity.

"By Jove! who arranged you in this guise, you and your cows?" I said to the poor devil, stopping before him.

He made a few grimaces before explaining; but the offer of a cigar, that rarely misses its effect, at last unloosed his tongue. He then told me that the Moonlighters had come with a razor to cut his ears, a week after having cut the tails of his cows as a warning.

"And what could have been the motive of such cowardly, barbarous mutilation?"

He had accepted work on a *boycotted* farm, though the League had expressly forbidden it; in other words, he was what the Irish call a "land-grabber."

"Where are you going with your cows?"

"To sell them at Listowel, if I may, which is not certain."

"Why is it not certain? Because they are unprovided with a tail? At the worst that would only prevent them being made into ox-tail soup," I say, trying to enliven the conversation by an appropriate joke.

"That's not it," answers the man. "But the interdict applies to the sale of the cows as well as to having any intercourse with me. I am forbidden to buy anything, and anyone speaking to me is fined two shillings."

He seemed to think this perfectly natural and even just, like the Leper of the "Cité d'Aoste," or like common convicts when one talks to them of their punishment.

"I gambled and I lost—so much the worse for me! . . ." all his resigned attitude seemed to say.

"Perhaps they don't know it yet in Listowel!" he resumed with a sigh, and hopefully pushed on with his cows.

"Have there been many cases of such agrarian mutilation in the country?" I ask MacMahon.

"No," said my guide. "Perhaps half a dozen or

so within the year.* They used to be much more numerous, but somehow they seem to go out of fashion under the sway of the League. But there are still other ways of annoying the enemy; fires are very frequent, so are blows, personal injuries, and even murder, threatening letters, and, above all, verbal intimidation."

Such proceedings, I understand, are altogether disowned by the chiefs of the League, who only patronise *boycotting*. Let a farmer, small or great, decline to enter the organisation, or check it by paying his rent to the landlord without the reduction agreed to by the tenantry, or take the succession of an evicted tenant on his holding, or commit any other serious offence against the law of land war, he is at once boycotted. That is to say, he will no longer be able to sell his goods, to buy the necessaries of life, to have his horses shod, his corn milled, or even to exchange one word with a living soul, within a circuit of fifteen to twenty miles round his house. His

---

* My guide was quite right. In a statistical table of trials between July, 1885, and July, 1886, for the County Kerry, I find the following items: *maiming cattle*, 9; *injury to person*, 7; *murders*, 3; *firing at persons*, 8; *firing into houses*, 15; *threatening letters*, 125; *intimidation*, 36; *malicious injury*, 22; *arson*, 19; *assaults*, 22. The above figures, it should be observed, only relate to outrages brought home to their authors; there can be no doubt that a much larger number of agrarian outrages remain unpunished.

servants are tampered with and induced to leave him, his tradespeople are made to shut their door in his face, his neighbours compelled to cut him. It is a kind of excommunication, social, political and commercial ; an interdict sometimes aggravated with direct vexations. People come and play football on his oat fields, his potatoes are rooted out, his fish or cattle poisoned, his game destroyed.

"But supposing that instead of bearing meekly such indignities, he shows a bold front, shoulders his gun and keeps watch ?"

"Then his business is settled. Some day or other, he will receive a bullet in his arm, if not in his head."

It will not perhaps be unnecessary to explain here the origin of that word *boycott*, so frequently used during the late few years. Everybody knows that on the British side of the Channel, but the French reader is not bound to remember it so exactly.

In September, 1881, at a mass meeting held in Clare County, Mr. Parnell almost without being aware of the importance of his words, advised his friends, to exclude from the pale of social life whoever should eject a tenant for reason of an unpaid rent, or take the succession of the evicted farmer.

The first application of that new penalty fell upon a certain Captain Boycott, a retired officer, who had applied himself to agriculture. Having had occasion to evict an obdurate defaulter, he saw himself within a few days forsaken by his servants, tabooed by his neighbours, reduced to dig out his own potatoes, and generally to become his own valet.

The affair produced great sensation. The whole press talked about it. Legions of reporters flocked to the spot to follow the phases of the war waged between Captain Boycott and his opponents. Upon a memorable occasion a regular army of Orangemen, 7000 strong, they say, came over from Ulster to give a lift to him and help him to get in the harvest which threatened to rot standing. But the place became too hot for Captain Boycott. He was obliged to give way at last and leave his place in Connaught. (By the way, he ultimately returned there, and is now quite popular.)

In the meanwhile his name, used as a proverb, or rather as a *verb*, has come to describe a way of intimidation, which at the hands of the League is a redoubtable weapon, more powerful than a hundred batteries of 100-ton guns.

"Could you show me anybody who is actually under boycott?"

"Could I? That will not be difficult. There! Mr. Kennedy, beyond that clump of trees. He has been boycotted eighteen months."

"Do you think I might call on him?"

"Certainly. But I shall ask leave to wait for you outside the gate, sir, on account of the League of course.——You may laugh at its verdict, not I."

Ten minutes later, I was at Mr. Kennedy's gate. A little country house rather decayed, in the middle of grounds which no gardener has seen for at least two years. Nobody in sight. I try the bell-rope. It remains in my hand. I am then reduced to an energetic tattoo on the plate which shuts the lower part of the gate.

Attracted by the unusual noise, a tall white-haired man makes his appearance at an upper window. Surprised at first, and even somewhat alarmed, he listens to my request, is reassured, and even comes to unbar the door. As I had hoped, he is not sorry to unloose his tongue a little, and with the best grace possible tells me the whole affair.

"Yes, I am boycotted for having, single among all his tenants, paid to my landlord the entire rent of those meadows you see yonder. How do I take my situation? Well, as a philosopher. At the beginning, I thought it inconvenient to be deprived of new bread, to do without meat, and worse still, to be left without servants. But I have learnt by degrees to accommodate myself to my new condition. I have made provisions for a siege. I have found a few servants, strangers to the district, and made my arrangements to send my butter to Cork by rail. On the whole, there is not much to complain of. I should, of course, prefer things to follow their usual course. It is tedious at times to find oneself out of the pale of humanity. But you end by discovering that solitude has its advantages. You develop accomplishments up to that time latent in you. For instance, I shoe my horses myself; I have learnt to set a window pane, to sweep a chimney. My daughters have improved in cooking. We eat a great many chickens; now and then we kill a sheep; when we want butcher-meat, we must send rather far for it. The same for beer, wine, and many other commodities. It *is* inconvenient—no more."

At Listowel; a market day. Great animation on the market-place; tongues are busy; whisky seems to be flowing freely at every tap-room and tavern.

But not much business is done, as far as I can judge. My guide calls my attention to two interesting phenomena that I should not, perhaps, have noticed otherwise.

The first is a man in breeches, with bare calves, a *shillelagh* under his arm, who seems to be a farmer in a small way. He approaches a wheel-barrow filled with big hob-nailed shoes, which a woman is dragging, and falls to examining them, evidently intent on buying a pair. Almost at the same moment, a boy of fifteen or sixteen comes to the other side of the woman and whispers something in her ear. She nods. At once the customer, turning very red in the face, lets go the pair of shoes and turns away. MacMahon says the man is a newly boycotted man and the boy an agent of the League, whose function consists in reporting the interdict to those who have not heard of it as yet.

The other phenomenon is more remarkable. It is a stout gentleman in a shooting-jacket, carrying a double-barrelled gun of the latest model, and followed by a constable who also carries his regulation gun. The stout gentleman stops before a door where a smart *outside car* with a servant in livery is waiting for him. He takes his seat; the constable jumps on after him. Is the stout gentleman under a writ of *habeas corpus*, I wonder, and is he going to be taken into the county jail? Not a bit of it. He is simply a landowner under threat of death, who has thought fit to indulge in a body-guard. He and the constable are henceforth inseparable.

A large tract of uncultivated land. It was farmed at £60 a year. The farmer was a sporting man, fond of races and the like. To simplify his work he had the whole property converted into pasture. But his expensive mode of living obliged him now and then to sell a few head of cattle. The hour came when he had not one calf left, and he found himself utterly incapable of paying his rent. He was evicted. Sure not to find another tenant, on account of the law laid down by the League that every evicted farm should be left unoccupied, the landlord had recourse to the only sort of *métayage* known in Ireland. (*Métayage*, it should be explained, is the kind of farming used in most French provinces, where the owner of the land enters into yearly partnership with his tenant, and advances the necessary capital in the shape of manure, seed, beasts of burden, and machinery, on the understanding that the crops be shared equally between himself and the tenant.)

To return to my Kerry landlord: he set up on his meadows a caretaker, with a salary of twenty-five shillings a week and forty cows to keep. At the end of the first month the tails of ten cows had been chopped off, while two of them had died from suspicious inflammation of the bowels. It became necessary to put the cows, and the caretaker as well, under the protection of a detachment of police. Cost: two pounds a week for each constable. Nett loss at the end of the half-year: £60. The landlord wisely judged that it would be much better to send his cows to the slaughter-house, to pay off caretaker and police, and to forget that he ever was a landowner.

In the same district, another farm gone waste. The tenant did not pay. He was evicted, but had another holding close by, where he encamped, and from that vantage-ground sent the following ultimatum to his *ci-devant* landlord:—"The hay I have left on my late farm is worth £30. I demand fifteen for allowing you to mow and sell it; you shall not see a shilling of it on any other terms." Fury of the landlord. Then he cools down, thinks better of it, offers ten pounds. The evicted tenant declines the offer; a whole army would not have brought him round. Meanwhile, the hay got rotten.

By the road-side near Castlemaine, is a row of barracks, where men, women, and children are huddled together. Those are *League-huts*, that is to say, a temporary shelter which the League offers to ejected tenants, for having, upon its command, declined to pay their rent. The cabins from which the poor wretches have been turned out, although they had, as a rule, built them themselves, are within shooting distance, on the right hand. They bear evident traces of having been fired by the sheriff's officers in order to make them uninhabitable, and they present the desolate aspect of homesteads adjoining a field of battle. Walls broken by the crowbar, doors ajar, rubbish and ruins everywhere. Is it politic on the part of the landlords to add the horrors of fire to those of eviction? Hardly so, the outsider will think. It adds nothing to the majesty of the law to wage war with inanimate things. The exercise of a right ought never to assume the appearance of an act of revenge. Wrongly or rightly, eviction by itself always bears an odious character; but to see the house you have built with your own hands burnt to the ground will ever seem to cry for vengeance to Heaven. And, after all, who is the gainer by such violence? The League. It takes care to retain the victims of eviction within sight of the scene of their woes, feeds them, harbours them, exhibits them as in an open museum, by the side of their destroyed homes. And it is a permanent, practical lesson for the passer-by, a realistic drama where the landlord appears torch in hand, while the League dries the tears of the afflicted and allows them £2 a week. That is the usual pay for one family.

CHAPTER IX.

A KERRY FARMER'S BUDGET.

"I wonder how landlords can manage to live, under such conditions," I said to my guide. "Are there any tenants left paying their rent?"

"There are many. First, those who have been able to come to an agreement with their landlord about the reduction of 20, 25, 30 per cent. that they claimed; in such cases the landlord's income is reduced, but at least he still retains a part of it. Then, there is the tenant's live stock; he cannot prevent its being seized for rent, in case of execution, and consequently chooses to pay, if possible, or he would have to sell his cattle to avoid distress, which means ruin to the family. Lastly, there are the tenants who pay secretly, although pretending to adhere to the rules of the League—*backsliders* they are called—a class more numerous than could be supposed at first sight."

Here MacMahon laughed. He went on:

"I will tell you, Sir, a story I have heard lately, of

a man in county Cork, who wanted to pay his landlord but dared not, on account of the other tenants on the estate. Coming across the landlord on a lone road (not improbably after many an unfruitful attempt for such a propitious opportunity) he stood before him in a threatening attitude. 'Put your hand in my coat's inside pocket!' he said gruffly. The landlord did not understand at first what the man meant, and considering his look and address, was far from feeling reassured. 'What do you mean?' he asked uneasily. 'I tell you, sir, put your hand in my coat's inside pocket, and feel for what you find in it.' At last the landlord did as he was bidden. He put his hand in the man's pocket, and extracted from it a bundle of papers, carefully tied up, that looked like banknotes. At once the tenant took to his heels. 'The devil a penny of rent you can ever say I paid you,' said he, in the same strange threatening tone of voice, as he ran away. Still, the banknotes in the landlord's hand were exactly to the amount of the rent due. As a rule, when the tenant is really able to pay his rent, he pays it."

Such has not been the general case, it seems, for the last three years. *In produce*, perhaps the Irish farmer might have paid his rent, as the crops have been, on the whole, fairly up to the average. In

A Kerry Farmer's Budget.

money, he cannot, because the fall of prices on hay, potatoes, beef, mutton, pork, and butter alike, in 1885, 1886, 1887, has been at least 20 per cent. on the former and average prices, which not only means no margin whatever of profit to the farmer, besides his necessary expenses, but in most cases the sheer impossibility of providing for the forthcoming outlay in seeds, manure, and labour.

This may not be self-evident. Many a reader probably fails to see why a fall of 20 per cent. on the prices of agricultural produce must necessarily entail a total disability to pay the rent. "I can well understand the demand of a proportional reduction of rent in such cases," he will say, "but not absolute non-payment." To fully realise the situation, one must go into the details of a farmer's life.

Let us take the case of Denis O'Leary, a Kerry man, with fourteen acres of good land. He seems to be in easy circumstances; his house is clean and pretty; he owns three cows, two sows, ten sheep, and about a score hens. Denis O'Leary is a good man, industrious and thrifty, who does all the work on his farm, with the help of wife and three children. He likes his pipe of tobacco, and on Sundays, a glass of beer over the counter with a friend or two, but otherwise indulges in no expensive habits. On the whole he can be considered a pattern tenant, as well as one of the most fortunate of his class. His rent, which had been gradually raised by his landlord up to the sum of £11 6s., was in 1883 put down at £8 7s. by the Land Commissioners.

Such being the case, when we are told that the same Denis O'Leary, who was for five years able to pay the larger rent, is now unable to pay the smaller one, this may look absurd. Still, it is the simple truth. To ascertain the fact, it is only necessary to make the budget of the O'Leary family.

The yearly expenditure, unavoidable and irreducible, is as follows:—

EXPENDITURE.

	£	s.
Taxes, rates, and county cess	1	15
Turf (Royalty on)	1	10
Clothing and shoes	6	10
Meat	2	15
Bread	6	18
Beer and tobacco	2	5
Oil, candles, sundries	2	15
Sugar and tea	6	5
School fees	0	7
Church subscription	0	10
Total	31	10

Most assuredly there is nothing excessive in such a budget of expenditure for a family of four. If even it is possible for Denis O'Leary not to go beyond its narrow limits, it is because he consumes in kind a large proportion of the produce of his fourteen acres, namely, some hundred stones of potatoes, with a good deal of milk, eggs, and butter. This alimentary deduction duly made, he has still a certain quantity of agricultural produce (which shall be supposed here a constant quantity) to sell, as follows :—

    1800 lbs. Potatoes.
    2200 ,, Wheat.
    1750 ,, Oats.
     38 ,, Wool.
    116 ,, Butter.
    1000 ,, Straw.
     25 dozen Eggs.
     3 Pigs.
     2 Calves.
     3 Lambs.

The above commodities have not, unfortunately, a constant value. They sell more or less, according to the fluctuations of prices on the market. In 1882, 1883, 1884, prices were high. Denis O'Leary's revenue was consequently as under :—

REVENUE (THREE YEARS AGO).

		£	s.
Sold : 1800 lbs. Potatoes		3	8
2200 ,, Wheat		9	0
1750 ,, Oats		6	4
38 ,, Wool		1	15
116 ,, Butter		5	7
1000 ,, Straw		1	5

	£	s.
25 dozen Eggs	1	2
3 Pigs	5	10
2 Calves	6	15
3 Lambs	3	5
Total	43	11

When Denis O'Leary had deducted from his revenue of £43 11s. the yearly expenditure of £31 10s., he had still £12 1s. left. He was able, accordingly, to pay £8 7s. rent (or even £11 6s. before the judicial reduction), and the rent duly paid, he was still the proud nett gainer of four shillings under the old *régime*, of £3 14s. under the new.

Unhappily, prices fell down in 1885, 1886, and 1887, to the tune of 25 or 30 per cent. on nearly all agricultural produce, with the exception perhaps of oats and eggs, so that the revenue of the O'Leary family (all things otherwise equal) has come to be as under:—

REVENUE (AT PRESENT).

		£	s.
Sold: 1800 lbs.	Potatoes	2	8
2200 ,,	Wheat	7	0
1750 ,,	Oats	6	2
38 ,,	Wool	1	5
116 ,,	Butter	3	12
1000 ,,	Straw	0	15
25 dozen	Eggs	1	5
3 Pigs		3	4
2 Calves		4	8
3 Lambs		2	10
Total		32	9

Thus, the revenue and expenditure are nearly equal, with a slight balance of nineteen shillings, that could hardly be proffered for rent. Local usurers are not wanting, of course, who will advance to Denis O'Leary the necessary funds, at 10 or 15 per cent., if he wants to pay the landlord, all the same. But then his budget is no more in a state of equilibrium: deficit enters it, to widen every year up to the final catastrophe. In other words, Denis O'Leary cannot pay the rent, unless he draws on his capital. One may well understand that he should not relish the idea, considering especially that the landlord's rack-rent has been reduced three years ago in the Land Court, and that the same landlord demurs to a fresh reduction, so obviously just and necessary that all landlords in England have granted it of their own free will these last three years.

And Denis O'Leary is a wonder in his class: he is an industrious, hard-working, wise man, without a penny of previous debt. He has precisely the area of land adequate to his means, and the live-stock indispensable to manure the soil. He does not drink, he does not gamble, he is never ill, he has no old people to support, he has not experienced failures or mishaps of any kind, and his crops are fairly up to the average.

Let us come back, however, to the world as it is, and see Man with his foibles, his usual neglects, errors, and mishaps. Let us suppose that he has more land on his hands than he can well manage to till, or that his holding, on the contrary, is too small for his wants. Let us suppose that instead of selling three pigs and two calves, he was not able to rear them, or lost them from disease; that instead of bringing to market 1,800 lbs. of potatoes he had to buy some hundredweight of the same for domestic consumption—the man is lost, irretrievably lost. Not only will he never be able to pay the landlord one farthing, but it will be enough that the crops should be slightly under the average to make a hopeless beggar of him—a case of outdoor or indoor relief for the parish.

Now, these are the circumstances of six or seven tenants out of ten in the lowlands of Kerry, where they seem to be comparatively well off. If we leave the plains for the higher districts bordering on the sea, the question is simpler still. There is no need of long accounts here. The hour of irretrievable misery has struck long ago, and habitual hunger stares us in the face.

UP IN THE MOUNTAINS.

The mountains of Kerry are the finest in the island. They form its south-western angle, throwing out on the Atlantic the peninsula of Dingle, between the bay of the same name and the Kenmare River. As you leave the plain following the Cahirciveen road towards the coast, you see them develop their parallel ranges, which are divided by deep valleys. Some of these valleys are fertile, being watered by impetuous streams from the mountain side. But the general impression one receives is that of agricultural poverty, as is the case in nearly all mountainous countries in the world. Pastures are thinner, cattle less numerous, homesteads fewer and more miserable than in the plain. Human creatures themselves partake of the general look of wretchedness that prevails. They live on potatoes, milk, and porridge; seldom eat bread, meat never; wine, beer, tea, coffee are to them unknown luxuries. Their ill-shaped cottages are made of soft stone, with a thatched roof maintained by ropes made of straw. There they all sleep on a bed of rushes, which they share with the pig, when there is such a thing, for even the traditional pig has become now a symptom of wealth in a manner. On the beams of the roof roost perhaps half-a-dozen hens and chickens.

Sloth and dirt hold here an undivided sway. Not a woman—and some are pretty—seems to mind the spots and holes in her garments; not one knows the use of soap or needle. They appear to have a rooted dislike for the comb; their hair falls on their back as is the fashion among the Australian aborigines, in nature's simple disorder.

Men look heavy and apathetic. They work as little as they can manage—one or two days out of seven, perhaps—and do not even think of seeking their sustenance from the sea, which is so close to them. The most they can do is to draw from it now and then a cart-load of seaweed to manure their miserable plot of ground. Their existence rolls on dull, idle, devoid of interest. It is the brute life in its most wretched and hideous state. Here is old Ireland as Gustave de Beaumont's admirable book showed it to us fifty years ago. Hardly do those wretched products of Anglo-Saxon civilization receive a faint echo of the outer world when the electoral time comes.

The consequence is that the agrarian crisis is reduced here to its simplest expression, *i.e.*, sheer impossibility to pay the rent because of total absence of the £ s. d. wherewith. Elsewhere that impossibility may be half assumed; it is certainly mixed in the plain with bad will, goaded in the peasant's heart by that dogged desire to possess the land which is so natural in him. In the mountain it is not a political fiction that holds the sway: famine is the king; and it is the spontaneous product of the very nature of things.

For the naturally infertile soil has reached here to such a degree of subdivision that it is no longer sufficient even to feed those it bears. The greater part of those wretched holdings of five or six acres are let at the nominal price of about £4, to which must be added the taxes, poor-rates, and county-cess, increasing it by a quarter or a third. Four, five, six, sometimes ten or twelve beings with human faces squat on that bit of worthless ground and till it in the most primitive manner. Money, tools, intelligence, pluck, all are wanting there. Viewing things in the most optimist light, supposing the year to have been an exceptionally good one, the potato crop to have been plentiful, the cow to have hunted out on the hill-side the necessary grass for the making of a little butter, all that will be sufficient perhaps to prevent starvation. But where will the money be found to pay Queen and landlord?

Let a child or an old person eat ever so little in the year, his food cannot but represent a value. Let that value be £4. Can six acres of mountain ground managed without skill or manure, render five, six, ten times £4 a year, and a rent in addition of five to six pounds? It is sheer impossibility.

A few examples.

James Garey, fifty years old, married, four children. Nominal rent £5 14s. Two cows, one pig, eight chickens. About six acres of land. Cultivates only part of it, about three acres, where he grows potatoes; the remainder is pasture. Sold this year thirty shillings' worth of butter; ate his potatoes from first to last; has not paid a farthing to his landlord for the last four years. Owes £6 to the draper-grocer; would never be able to pay his taxes if two of his children, who are out in domestic situations, did not send him the necessary amount to prevent execution.

Widow Bridget Molony, sixty years old; five children; seven acres of land. Nominal rent £6 12s. Four cows, an eighteen-month-old calf, two pigs, twenty chickens. Sold £3 10s. of butter this year, £2 oats, 15 shillings potatoes, and a pig for £3; just sent a calf to market, offering it for £1 15s.; did not find purchaser. Thinks herself relatively lucky, as she is owing only two years' rent to her landlord. Two of her children have situations at Liverpool, and help her to pay the taxes.

Thomas Halloran, forty years. Three children,

A Kerry Farmer's Budget.

eight acres of land; rent £6 15s. Two cows, fifteen sheep, a pig, an ass, twelve chickens. Sold during the year ten shillingsworth of butter and ten sheep at twelve shillings a head. Has paid nothing to landlord since November, 1884.

Michael Tuohy, seventy years old, three children, four grandchildren. Nine acres of land, £7 rent. A cow and five hens. Can no longer afford a pig. Sold only fifteen shillingsworth of butter this year, and had to get rid of two cows out of three to pay the ten per cent interest of a debt he has contracted with the National Bank. Owes four years' rent to his landlord; hopes that his son, who has emigrated to the United States, will send him the money for the taxes; if the son doesn't, he cannot see any way to save the last cow.

Examples of that description could be multiplied *ad infinitum;* they are, so to say, the rule in the mountainous districts, where the holdings are for the most part beneath £10 rent, and totally unequal even to sustain the farmer.

Glenbeigh, between Kilarglin and Cahirciveen. This place was the theatre of several deplorable scenes in January last, on Mr. R. Winn's property.

That property, very extensive, but consisting of poor, not to say totally barren land, was put down at £2000 on the valuation roll. The aforesaid rent not having been paid during four or five years, the owner was of course in very strait circumstances; he had to go to some Jews, who substituted themselves in his place, and undertook to enforce payment. But the extreme poverty of the tenants proved even stronger than the energetic tribe. In consequence of the gradual subdivision of the land, they had come to hold diminutive scraps of it such as could not even grow the potatoes sufficient for their sustenance. After various judicial skirmishes, the plain result of which was to establish the utter incapacity of the peasants to give a penny, the council of creditors resolved in the depth of winter to undertake a wholesale campaign of evictions. Seventy-nine writs of ejectment were issued, and soon after the undersheriff, backed by a strong detachment of mounted constables, arrived to evict the wretched families.

The operations began at a certain Patrick Reardon's, on a literally barren land, for which he was expected to pay £4 10s. a year. He was the father of eight children, but did not even possess a pig, not a pair of chickens. The furniture consisted of a bed, a rickety table and a kettle. Squatting on the ground with his whole family, according to the time-honoured custom, he waited for the executors of the law. Requested to pay, he answered that he possessed not one farthing; he was then informed that they were going to set fire to his cabin, in order to oblige him to evacuate the premises. The act soon followed the threat. A lighted match applied to the thatched roof, and in a few minues the whole was in conflagration. All the neighbouring populations, who had run on to the scene of the tragedy, saluted the dreadful deed with hooting and execration.

The myrmidons of the law pursued nevertheless the execution of their mandate. They went next to the dwelling of another tenant, Thomas Burke, inscribed on the list of debtors for a sum of £20. He had five children, and, like the above-mentioned, not one farthing to offer to the creditors. Order was given to set fire to his roof, but it was found to be so damp that fire would not take; so they had to attack the walls with the crowbar and pick-axe. The miserable inmates appeared then to the eyes of the indignant crowd, half naked, wan, emaciated, and starved; and so heartrending was the scene that with difficulty the representative of the League (who had come there for that very purpose) prevented the mob from stoning the bailiffs to death.

Then came the turn of the third cottage. Two old men lived in it, Patrick and Thomas Diggin. The family of the former included ten persons ; that of the latter, six. They owed a rent of £8, and had not a shilling between them all. Patrick's wife, however, came forward, and declared she had just received £2 from her daughter, who was a servant in Belfast. Would they accept that, and stop the execution ? The under-sheriff, whom the duties of his office oblige to back the bailiffs, urged them to accept the touching offer. They refused, and set fire to the roof. Then Patrick Diggin, an eighty-year-old man, was seen coming out of his home sobbing ; he was followed by all his children and grandchildren. By an irresistible impulse of sympathy all crowd round him, offering what little they possess to the relief of that misery. The constables themselves, moved almost to tears, contribute their silver coin to the subscription which has been spontaneously organized. To carry the barbarous work further becomes an impossibility. The sheriff's substitute gives the signal for departure, and the cavalcade follows amidst the derisive cries of the multitude.

All those poor people, except one family, have since been re-installed on their holdings, and are now at work on their farms—a strange evidence of the uselessness and cruelty of eviction, to make tenants pay who cannot.

VALENTIA ISLAND.

At Cahirciveen, I crossed the strait which divides the main land from the island of Valentia. This is the extreme point of the old continent, where the Transatlantic cables are placed. Good, honest, plucky fellows! what repose after the misery of Kerry! I am speaking of the fishermen of the island, a peculiar race who never ploughed any fields but those of the ocean. Every night they risk their lives on the giant billows, and earn their bread valiantly. They know nothing of sheep rot, potato disease, or landlordism; all they know is the management of their boats, the making and mending of their nets, and the art of making the deep yield food for their young. Strangers to the neighbouring world, they ignore even its language, and only talk the rude idiom of their ancestors, the Irish of the time of the O'Donoghue.

Noble fellows! I shall not soon forget the night I spent there watching them as they were fishing between the Skellings, two enormous rocks that rise like Gothic cathedrals, about twelve miles from Bray Head, and on which the waves are eternally breaking with a thundering noise. My guide had warned me against offering them money; it would offend them, he said, so I did not do it. I simply drank with them a glass of whisky when they prepared to go home towards daybreak, the stars still shining. And, comparing their happy courage with the distress of Kerry, I wished them from the bottom of my heart never to become acquainted with agriculture on small holdings, under an English landlord.

CHAPTER X.

RURAL PHYSIOLOGY.

We have glanced at a few facts presenting symptoms of the Irish disease, which were taken as chance guided us, in a ride through a south-western county. Similar symptoms are everywhere to be found through the island. To appreciate them at their right value, as even to comprehend them, it is essentially requisite to know, at least in its broader outlines, the physiology of landed property in this entirely agricultural country.

Vast landed property and parcelled-out culture. This is the epitome of such a physiology. At the base of the social edifice we find the tenant, generally a Catholic and of indigenous race, occupying and cultivating after his own fashion the thousandth or ten thousandth part of a property ranging over an area of some hundred thousand acres. At the summit we find the landlord, almost invariably of English and Protestant race, ruling by right of primogeniture over this immense space.

Does this right rest at its origin on confiscation and spoliation, as is averred by the Irish? That is of little importance from a legal point of view, for prescription has covered the spoliation by an occupation of two to eight centuries. It is of far greater importance from a moral point of view, because that grievance, ill or well founded, serves as a handle for all agrarian recriminations.

In three out of five cases (so it has been shown by recent statistics) the landlord is an *absentee*, that is to say, he does not reside on his property, nor even in the kingdom, and spends abroad the money he raises on his lands. His income, from that source alone, is sometimes enormous—£10,000 a year—(Lord Greville, Westmeath; Lord Carisford, Wicklow; Mr. Wandesford, Kilkenny; Mr. King, Longford; Lord Inchiquin, Clare); £16,000 a year—(Lord Claremont, Louth; Mr. Naper, Meath; Lord Leconfield, Clare; Lord Ventry, Kerry); £26,000 and £32,000 a year—(Duke of Abercorn, Tyrone; Marquis of Clanricarde, Galway; Lord Kenmare, Kerry); £40,000, £80,000, and even £120,000 a year—(Mr. MacDonnell, Kildare; Marquis of Coningham, Cavan, Clare, and Donegal; Marquis of London-

Rural Physiology.

derry, Down; Marquis of Downshire, &c.). Rent rolls of £4,000, £3,000, and £2,000 a year too plentiful to be mentioned.

Three-fifths at least of those sums are lost every year for Ireland, and they go out of the island without having in any way helped to increase her capital in agricultural machinery, live stock, and general improvements of the land. As a natural consequence, the soil is ill-cultivated, ill-manured, insufficiently covered with cattle. For centuries its energies have suffered a constant draining, and nothing has been done to repair its losses.

That soil has a tendency to subdivision in the hands of the tenants, who cultivate it by truly pre-historic methods. The figures are given in round numbers as follows:—

Against 24,000 holdings of a value of above £500 a year there are in Ireland 85,000 holdings producing from £25 to £500 a year; 49,000 from £12 to £29 a year; 77,000 from £8 to £12 a year; 196,000 from £4 to £8 a year; lastly, 218,000 holdings of a revenue of *under £4 a year.*

That is to say, out of six or seven hundred thousand families, living exclusively upon the product of the soil, more than two-thirds must get their sustenance from a wretched bit of ground, estimated by the owner himself at a value of £4 to £8 a year!

To state such an economical paradox is to denounce it. Where there is nothing, the landlord, like the king, loses his rights. The situation, then, would already be strangely anomalous, even if the respective titles of landlord and tenant were of the clearest and most transparent kind. But it is complicated in Ireland by the most curious conceptions and customs in matters of landed property.

To understand those conceptions and customs, a Frenchman must begin by putting aside all his Latin ideas. With us, since the Convention, one can always know by the Survey-Rolls to whom belongs absolutely such or such a piece of land. He who owns it is free to sell it, to give it, to let it as he pleases. His right is absolute; it is the right of "use and abuse," according to the forcible expression of the Roman code. It passes with this absolute character to sons, grandsons, or legatees.

In Ireland it is feudal law that obtains still; an estate is not a property, it is a fief. The lord of that estate is not the proprietor of it, he is an usufructuary, as it were, a life-tenant on it. He has only a limited right to his own land. He cannot sell it without the written consent of his substitute in the entail, and the authorization of the persons, often countless in numbers, that have some hereditary right on his property at the same time with him; most of the estates are encumbered with perpetual rents, served out either to the younger branches of the family, to old servants, or to creditors. All the titulary is free to alienate is his life interest, through some insurance combination with transfer of income.

If we add that the said titulary is generally absent from his property, that he does not manage it personally, and that in many cases he does not even exactly know where it is to be found, we must own that it is no wonder he is considered as a stranger.

A stranger he is besides, in race, by habits, by religion, by language. And yet this stranger,—precisely because his fief, practically inalienable, as it is immovable in its limits, has always been transmitted from father to eldest son in the family,—this stranger, of whom often nothing is known beyond his name, has a story, true or legendary, attached to him and to his title. It matters little that the revenue of the estate was scattered over five hundred heads, in the course of ten generations; the estate remains, and weighs on him with all its weight. We do not speak here of a mere geographical expression, of an area a hundred times parcelled out, altered, disfigured, in less than a century, but of land that for a thousand years, maybe, has changed neither form nor aspect.

At night, by the fireside, old people will recall how in former days this land was the collective property of the clan; how they were defrauded by a political chief that treacherously gave it up to the English, in order to receive investiture from their hands; how, following the fortunes of twenty successive rebellions and repressions, it was confiscated, sequestered, given anew, till it came to the actual landlords. A special literature, ballads, popular imagery, little books, and penny papers constantly harp on that ancient spoliation. It is the only history studied under thatched roofs. The peasant breathes it in the atmosphere, imbibes it by all his pores.

Convinced that he has a hereditary right to the domain in general, the Irish peasant besides attributes to himself a special and prescriptive right to the plot of ground that he, like the landlord, occupies from father to son, though on a precarious tenure. This right is not purely imaginary; it was consecrated in the year 1860 by a special Act of Parliament, due to the initiative of Mr. Gladstone. Recognised from immemorial times in Ulster, it has always been claimed in all the other parts of Ireland; it is the *tenant right*, what in our own Picardy is called the *droit de marché*.

It is well known in what consist this ancient prerogative of the Picardy farmer (Troplong in the Preface to his *Traité du Louage*, and Lefort in his *Histoire des contrats de location perpétuelle*, have treated it exhaustively): it is simply the privilege of preserving in perpetuity for him and for his heirs, the use of the ground for which he pays rent regularly.

Not only is this privilege not denied to him, but he can transfer it to a third person, for a premium that goes by the name of *intrade*. The amount of that premium is often a third or even a half of the intrinsic value of the soil. Formerly this "*droit de marché*" applied to everything that can be let or hired; the labourers, the threshers, the shepherds of a domain, each claimed it in his own province as a hereditary monopoly. In modern days it is strictly limited to the hiring of servants, in the few districts where it survived the French revolution (in Péronne for instance).

The thing that is only a curious exception in France has remained the rule in Ireland, where *tenant right* has been in force for the last twenty-seven years. And what, after all, can be better founded than such a right? Has not the tenant, in the majority of cases, made his plot of ground what it is? Has he not tilled it, improved it, manured it, drained it according to his better knowledge; in a word, has he not *created* it in its actual form?

"Let us," says the peasant, "admit the rights of the landlord. How could he deny me mine? Are they not legibly written in the furrow I have traced upon this earth, in the fruits I have made her bear? . . . The land is not a simple material, unreducible like a piece of gold. It is a chemical product, a conglomerate that is valuable especially by reason of all the substances I have mixed up with it during an occupation of ten, twenty, thirty years, or even more. . . . Who shall dare to deny the share I have brought into this company of which I am the acting manager, and deny that this share belongs to me?"

Such a theory would doubtless appear sheer lunacy to the French proprietor who has paid for his land £400 per hectare, and who has let it for a fixed period at a fixed price, with the understanding that at the end of the contract he shall find it in good condition and shall then do what he pleases with it. That theory, however, is so well suited to Ireland, where custom has the force of law, that the landlord does not even think, practically, of disputing the *tenant's right*.

As a rule he is only too glad to let his land to the farmers who have traditionally occupied it, on condition that they pay the usual rent.

But in practice, the Land Act of 1860, apparently so much in favour of the tenant, has produced disastrous effects. In the first place, by consecrating the right of the tenant only on improvements and enlargements made *with the landlord's consent*. Thence the consequence that not only is the landlord never willing to spend a farthing on the improvements of the land, but also that he systematically opposes them, for fear he should have to pay for them in the end. Besides many landlords have signed their new leases only after the farmer has given them a formal renunciation to the tenant right; or else they have taken advantage of the pretext that offered itself, and raised the rent by way of compensation against all risks. Lastly, in many a place where this right has become positive, the rural usurers alone have profited by it by discounting it to the peasantry.

The consequence is that the tenant right is often reduced practically to the implicit acknowledgment of the right of the farmer to occupy the land, so long as he pays his rent. It even happens not unfrequently that there is no lease and the occupancy goes on indefinitely without title. Doubtless this gives it only more value in the eyes of the peasant, naturally inclined to associate this absence of scrivening with the acknowledgment of his traditional rights.

Having been able in certain cases to sell or hire his "interest," he feels the more inclined to think himself entitled to divide it between his children. That division has become the rule, and what was once a farm of thirty to fifty acres turns out, at the third generation, parcelled in ten or twelve scraps of three to five acres. The landlord might have interfered in the beginning; he might have prevented such a division; he did not do it. Beside, that division of the land is recorded nowhere, has been the occasion of no formal deed; one member of the family answers for all the others, if necessary. How is one to unravel those private arrangements? And, after all, what does it matter, so long as the rents come in?

They come in during ten, during twenty years. Then the harvest is bad, or the sub-dividing of the soil has arrived at the last limit compatible with the needs of those that cultivate it. The rent is no longer paid, and then the difficulties begin. How is one to appraise the improvements introduced in the land by the actual possessor, or by his forefathers? How can one find out what is due to him, even with the best intentions? Is the landlord to give him an indemnity before he evicts him? But then it means ruin to the landlord, who will have to pay precisely because he has not been paid himself. It is the squaring of the circle. When only very small holdings are in question, the difficulty is generally met by remaining in *statu quo*. But supposing the debt to be more important, or to have been transferred to a third person, which is often the case, the question becomes insoluble.

Let us repeat that we must not consider these things from a French point of view. With us the idea of individual property is always of the clearest and simplest. The frequent sales and buying of land contribute still to make this idea of more actual and definite meaning to us. An hectare of grass or vine is, like any other goods, a merchandise that passes from hand to hand, and remains with the highest bidder. In Ireland the sales are rare, and in no case is it a question of absolute ownership; it is only a question about the respective and contradictory rights, some for life, some perpetual, some positive, others customary, of several persons over the same space of land, a space not to be transferred, not to be seized, and not to be fractionised. Is it any wonder that such contradictory pretensions should give rise to constant conflicts?

Everything concurs to shut in that rural world in a vicious circle. Not only does the peasant lack capital to improve his farming, but, assured of seeing his rent raised if he ventured on the least improvement, he is careful to make none. On his side the landlord, for dread of annoying contestations, opposes as much as lies in his power any amendment susceptible of being turned into a title for his tenant.

Is there a succession of relatively good harvests? He immediately raises the rent. Are the following years bad? He refuses to return to the old rate, in principle at least, because he finds it inconvenient to curtail a revenue to which he has accustomed himself, because he does not like to appear to bow before the League, and also because, being liable to expropriation, he is unwilling to depreciate beforehand the value of his property, which is always valued according to its rent.

Lastly, the holdings, being too often mere plots of ground, are hardly sufficient to keep the peasant and his family occupied, and do not always give him a sufficiency of food. And just because it is so, the unlucky wretch does not find work outside sufficient for the equilibrium of his poor finances. The class of agricultural labourers can hardly be said to exist in numerous districts, because everyone is a small farmer. The tenant then becomes completely sunk in his inaction; he becomes apathetic, and from a sluggard too often turns into a drunkard. His wife is ignorant and careless. She can neither sew, nor is she able to give a palatable taste to his monotonous fare. His children are pallid and dirty. Everything is sad, everything is unlovely around him; and, like a dagger festering in the wound, the thought that all his misery is due to the English usurper ever makes his heart bleed.

To all these causes of poverty and despair must be added the general difficulties that weigh on agriculture in all countries of Europe, the lowered prices of transport, the clearings of land in America and Australia, the awful transatlantic competition, the disease of potatoes. . . . The picture being finished, one thing only surprises—it is to find one single Irish farmer left in the country.

These explanations, with many others, were given me by a person that it is time I should introduce to the reader; for he is the incarnation of one of the essential wheels in the machinery of Irish landed property—Captain Pembroke Stockton, *land agent*.

The captain is a small fair man, of slim figure, of military aspect, who received me this morning at an office where he employs half a dozen clerks. The room was lined with green-backed ledgers, or, to speak more exactly, with rows of tin boxes, of a chocolate colour. To-night he receives me in a pleasant villa, where he takes me in his phaeton, drawn by two magnificent horses. He may be about fifty-three years old. His calm, regular-featured countetenance owes its peculiar character to the line that cuts his forehead transversely, and divides it into two parts, one white, the other bronzed by the sun; a mark left by the English forage-cap, which is like a small muffin, and is worn on one side of the head. The captain has seen service in India; he fought against Nana-Sahib, and even hung with his own hand a certain number of rebels, as he not unfrequently relates after dinner. He sold out when about thirty-five years of age, at a period when selling out still existed (in 1869), and got for his commission £3200, which, besides a small personal competency, allowed him to marry a charming girl, dowerless, according to the excellent English habit; children came: means became too straitened, and, to enlarge them, he resolved to become a *land agent*.

The land agent has no equivalent in France, except for house property. He is neither a notary, nor a steward, and yet he partakes of both, being the intermediary between landlord and tenant. It is he that draws up the leases and settlements; he who receives the rents, who sends out summons, who signs every six months the cheque impatiently expected by the landlord; he who represents him at law, he who negotiates his loans, mortgages, cessions of income, and all other banking operations. In a word, he is the landlord's prime minister, the person who takes on his shoulders all the management of his affairs, and reduces his profession to the agreeable function of spending money. The land agent naturally resides as a rule in the vicinity of the estate. Therefore he knows everybody by name; knows all about the incumbrances, the resources of every tenant, the length and breadth of every field, the price of produce, the probable value of the harvest; all the threads are in his hands; the landlord counts upon him, approves everything he does, upholds his rigours, and submits to his tolerance. Is he not himself at his mercy? The agent keeps all his deeds of property; has personally written out every one of them; knows, in fact, a great deal more than himself about it.

Let us premise that very considerable interests are in question, and that the rents are ciphered by thousands of pounds sterling. It is easy to understand that the agent must be not only a man of honour, a clever man, a business man, but above all a man presenting the most serious guarantees from a financial point of view.

That is sufficient to imply that they are not counted by dozens in every district; and that a land agent provided with all the necessary qualifications must before long govern all the principal estates in a county. From his office, situated in the principal county-town, he rules over ten, twenty, or thirty, square miles of land, cultivated by five or six thousand farmers, under some twenty landlords.

Thence the natural consequence that the same policy generally prevails in all the administration of the landed property in one district. The personal character of the landlord may, indeed, influence it in some ways, but the character of the agent is of far greater importance. And thence this other consequence, not less serious for the farmer, and which gives the key to many an act of agrarian violence,—that in case of open war, in case of eviction especially, it is not only an affair between the landlord and the tenant, but also between the tenant and all the landlords in his county, through their one representative.

Has he been evicted? It will be well-nigh impossible for him to get another farm in this county, where he was born, where his relations are living, where he has all his habits, all his roots, as it were. And no work to be had outside agricultural work. . . . Emigration only is open to him,—which is equivalent to saying that eviction must necessarily be followed by transportation.

Let us imagine all the owners of houses in Paris, bound together in association, to be in the hands of a single agent; let us suppose that a dweller in one of those houses is turned out of it for quarrelling with his *concierge* or for any other reason, and unable to find a house to live in; we shall then have an idea of the state of mind in which eviction places the Irish peasant. Let us add that this peasant has generally built with his own hand the hut that is taken from him; let us add that for him it is not only a question of knowing whether he shall have a roof over his head, but a question of being able to live by the only trade he has learnt.

For many other reasons, the question of agencies on a large scale still contributes to make the problem more intricate.

In all affairs personal intercourse brings an element the importance of which must not be overlooked. A man will display the greatest inflexibility in writing, who will hesitate to do so face to face with his opponent. If the landlord knew his tenants, if he lived among them, if he entered into their life and saw their misery, very often, may be, he would recoil before barbarous rigours, while the agent, by his very profession is obliged to act with the precision of a guillotine. The influence of women, so gentle and conciliatory, is absent from the system. Pity, sympathy, human contact, have no part in it. Can we wonder if harmony be destroyed?

Examples are not wanting to show that a different system, a policy of gentleness, of direct and mutual concessions, and well directed efforts, bear very different results. I shall quote as an instance the case of an English lady, Miss Sherman Crawford, who bought, some twenty years ago, at a legal sale, a small half-ruined estate in Ireland. She went to live on it, and began by giving her ten or twelve tenants a written promise that they would get the benefit of all their improvements without having cause to fear that the rent should be raised. Then she made it a rule that everyone should come directly to her in case of difficulties, and not to an agent.

She built a few sheds, repaired two or three cottages, on occasions lent a five pound note to facilitate the buying of a cow or pig. That was enough. In spite of the difference in race, religion, and language, she and her peasantry are on perfect terms with each other; her property of Timoleague thrives in the midst of general poverty and wretchedness; not an inch of ground lies uncultivated; the soil is well manured, well drained, well used; the people are happy and contented. To perform that miracle, all that was wanted was a little willingness, a little good management and gentleness.

But then Miss Crawford's property is neither too large nor too small. She brings there the capital needed, and allows it to circulate in the place. She sees everything with her own eyes, not with the eyes of an agent. She is not the titulary of an entailed estate, and has not given up its income to usurers. Her farms are large enough to allow her tenants to find their sustenance on them, for themselves and their families. In a word, her property is in everything the reverse of what is seen in all other parts of the island.

And in truth, if delirious legislators had proposed to themselves the task of inventing a system of landed property that would give neither security to the owner nor peace to the tenant, where could they have succeeded better than with the Irish system? It is at once stupid and ferocious, absurd and monstrous. How true, alas! that human genius, so well able sometimes to profit by natural forces, excels also in sterilizing them, in making them homicides!

CHAPTER XI.

EMIGRATION.

BEFORE setting foot in this country your notions are not unfrequently ready made about the characters of the inhabitants. You have gathered them from miscellaneous reading, novel-reading mostly, and what you expect is an Ireland poor certainly, but nevertheless gay, improvident, chivalrous, addicted to sound drinking, good eating, fond of practical jokes, not unmixed with riot and even blows; an Ireland, in short, such as Charles Lever and Carleton, Banim and Maxwell, Sam Lover and Thackeray have described; an Ireland where wit and humour are to be met at every step, where the last beggar has his little joke, where originality of thought, unexpectedness of action, fun inexhaustible, combine to form that eccentricity of manner which is ever associated with the idea of an Irishman.

That such an Ireland was, not long ago, a reality, one cannot doubt. A whole literature, a rich collection of tales, novels and legends is there to witness to the fact. Its historical existence is as scientifically demonstrated as that of our "Régence." The worldly exploits of the Duke of Richelieu are not better proved. But it is in vain you look to-day for that gay and careless Ireland; from Cape Clear to Malin Head, from Dublin to Galway, there is no vestige of it. She is dead and gone. Like Mr. Credit, bad payers have killed her. Between her and us there has been a great financial cataclysm where she has been wrecked: the *crash* of the great famine of 1846—1847.

Never did she rise from it. Forty years ago she contrived to exist somehow. The tenants were poor, to be sure, but the landlords were not, and they spent their money grandly. They led the usual life of rich country gentlemen, had large retinues of servants and horses, kept playing, drinking, and betting till they had only debts left, which course had at least the advantage of permitting their cash to circulate about the country. The local traffic was relatively large then. Butchers, coach-makers, wine-merchants, and horse-dealers made rapid fortunes. Few towns in Europe showed so much animation as Dublin, now so empty and so dull a place. Everybody was in debt with everybody: not one property was not mortgaged. It was the fashion at that time to pay only at the last extremity. A general complicity gave force of law to that habit. Lawsuits, of course, were plentiful, but what is there in a lawsuit to prevent a jolly squire from drinking hard, riding his horses at a break-neck pace, or galloping from morning till night behind his hounds?

Then came the potato-disease; then the famine, which brought in two years a general liquidation. Everyone awoke to find himself ruined; there were in six months fifty thousand evictions. The largest fortunes, when they escaped the Encumbered Estates Court, established in 1849, remained loaded with such heavy burdens that the income of the titulary fell to nothing. One was obliged to pinch then, to sell the horses, and shut up the kennel. There was an end to fun, and if there remained here and there some inveterate boon companion who would not give up the good old customs, the *Moonlighters* soon brought him to reason, poisoning his dogs and hunters, confiscating his arms, and at times mistaking the landlord for the game.

There is no vestige left now of the easy-going ways of old. The large town-houses and country seats are deserted or let to strangers; the cellar is empty, the dining-room silent. A gust of hatred and misery has blown on the isle and left all hearts frozen.

As for the peasant, the poor creature has too many cares for thinking of a joke now. Perhaps in other climes, under a clearer sky and warmer sun, he would revive, and find in his very distress the element for some witticism. But here, the damp atmosphere, united with persevering ill-fortune, has deluged and drowned for ever his Celtic good-humour. Hardly does he find now and then a glimpse of it at the bottom of an ale-jug or in the tumult of some election riot. If a quick repartee, one of his characteristic sallies, escapes him now, it is always bitter, and reminds you of the acrid genius of Swift.

"How deliciously pure and fresh is the air in Dublin," said Lady Carteret, the Lord Lieutenant of Ireland's wife, to the author of "Gulliver."

"For goodness' sake, Madam, don't breathe a word about it to the English. They would put a duty on it."

And his terrible satire about the famous "excess of population," that favourite hobby of economists, who has not it in mind?

"It is a melancholy object to those who walk through this great town or travel in the country, where they see the streets, the roads, and cabin-doors crowded with beggars of the female sex, followed by three, four, or six children, all in rags and importuning every passenger for an alms . . . I think it is agreed by all parties that this prodigious number of children . . . . is in the present deplorable state of the kingdom a very great additional grievance; and therefore, whosoever could find out a fair, cheap, and easy method of making these children sound, easy members of the commonwealth, would deserve so well of the public as to have his statue set up for a preserver of the nation. I shall now, therefore, humbly propose my own thoughts; which I hope will not be liable to the least objection.

" I have been assured by a very knowing American of my acquaintance in London that a young healthy child, well nursed, is, at a year old, a most delicious, nourishing, and wholesome food, whether stewed, roasted, baked, or boiled; and I make no doubt that it will equally serve in a fricassée or a ragout.

" I do therefore humbly offer it to public consideration that of the hundred and twenty thousand children already computed, twenty thousand may be reserved for breed, whereof one-fourth part to be males . . . . that the remaining hundred thousand may, at a year old, be offered in sale to the persons of quality and fortune through the kingdom; always advising the mother to let them suck plentifully in the last month so as to render them plump and fat for good tables. A child will make two dishes at an entertainment for friends, and when the family dines alone, the fore or hind quarter will make a reasonable dish, and, seasoned with a little pepper or salt, will be very good boiled on the fourth day, especially in winter.

"I have reckoned, upon a medium, that a child just born will weigh twelve pounds, and in a solar year, if tolerably nursed, will increase to twenty-eight pounds.

"I have already computed the charge of nursing a beggar's child (in which list I reckon all cottagers, labourers, and four-fifths of the farmers) to be about two shillings per annum, rags included; and I believe no gentleman would refuse to give two shillings for the carcase of a good fat child, which, as I have said, will make four dishes of excellent nutritive meat. Those who are more thrifty (as I must confess the times require) may flay the carcase: the skin of which, artificially dressed, will make admirable gloves for ladies and summer boots for fine gentlemen.

"As to our city of Dublin, shambles may be appointed for this purpose in the most convenient parts of it; and butchers we may be assured will not be wanting; although I rather recommend buying the children alive, then dressing them hot from the knife, as we do roasted pigs . . . .

"I think the advantages, by the proposals I have made, are obvious and many, as well as of the highest importance: for first, as I have already observed, it would greatly lessen the number of papists, with whom we are yearly overrun, being the principal breeders of the nation, as well as our most dangerous enemies . . . . Whereas the maintenance of a hundred thousand children, from two years old and upwards, cannot be computed at less than ten shillings a piece per annum, the nation's stock will be thereby increased fifty thousand pounds per annum, beside the profit of a new dish introduced to the tables of all gentlemen of fortune in the kingdom, who have any refinement in taste. And all the money will circulate among ourselves, the goods being entirely of our own growth and manufacture . . . . Besides, this would be a great inducement to marriage, which all wise nations have either encouraged by rewards or enforced by laws and penalties."

The grim sarcasm goes on in the same sinister, pitiless way up to the conclusion, which is worth the rest:

"I profess in the sincerity of my heart that I have not the least personal interest in endeavouring to promote this necessary work, having no other motive than the public good of my country, by advancing our trade, providing for infants, relieving the poor, and giving some pleasure to the rich. I have no children by which I can propose to get a single penny; the youngest being nine years old, and my wife past child-bearing."

Modern Philanthropy is not quite so bold as the Dean of St. Patrick in suggesting remedies for the relief of the sufferings of Ireland. Its great panacea is emigration. The first thing which attracts the eye in villages and boroughs is a large showy placard representing a ship in full sail, with the following words in large capitals, "Emigration! . . . . free passage to Canada, Australia, New Zealand! . . . . free passage and a premium to emigrants for Queensland! . . . ."

Technical particulars follow; the agents' addresses, the names of the outward-bound ships, &c. . . . . These placards are everywhere. At each turning, on every wall they stare you in the face, and fascinate the starving man. Numerous and powerful emigration companies paid by colonies where hands are wanting, patronized by all that is influential in the kingdom, work unremittingly in recruiting that army of despair for a voluntary transportation. And thus

Emigration. 185

a continuous stream of Irishmen is ebbing out through all the pores of the country.

Shall we give the official figures? There are none given unfortunately for the years between 1847 and 1851, corresponding to the "famine clearances" or famine evictions. All that is known is that at that time the population of Ireland suddenly decreased by one million six hundred and twenty-two thousand inhabitants, without it being possible to say how many had died of starvation, how many had embarked pell-mell on hundreds of ships, how many had perished at sea, how many had survived. Since 1851 the accounts are clear. It is known that 148,982 emigrants left Ireland in the eight last months of that year; 189,092 in 1852; 172,829 in 1853; 139,312 in 1854. During the following years the emigration slackens its pace by degrees and falls to the rate of 75,000 heads a year. It rises again in 1863—64, and attains the figure of over 105,000. Then it settles again to its level: 60,000, where for a time it remains stationary. Since 1880 it has risen again to 95,000, and over 100,000.

Within thirty years, the period included between the 1st of May, 1851, and the 1st of May, 1881, Ireland has lost through emigration alone *two million five hundred and thirty-six thousand six hundred and twenty-seven* of her children. The total for the last five years has not yet been published, but it certainly reaches half a million. From the year 1851, therefore, at least *three million* Irish people of both sexes have left the island, that is to say, nearly the half of a population then reduced to six-and-a-half million souls.

Has, at least, the result of that frightful exodus been to eradicate pauperism? One would like to believe it. Theorists had promised it. But alas! stern statistics are there to answer their fallacies.

Statistics inform us that the Ireland of 1887, with its present population, inferior to that of London, is poorer than it was in 1841, when it numbered eight million inhabitants. Twenty years ago the number of individuals admitted to workhouses was 114,594 out of six miilion inhabitants. To-day it is 316,165 out of a population diminished by a third. In 1884 the poor who received relief at home were 442,289. They are now 633,021. In other words, *one Irishman out of four* lives on public charity—when he lives at all.

Upon such facts, would you guess what monstrous conclusion the votaries of emigration at any price have come to? Simply this: that the blood-letting is not sufficient ; that Ireland must be drained of another million inhabitants. Such is Lord Salisbury's opinion. As if an area of 20,194,602 statute acres, so favoured geographically, was not calculated to nourish twelve or fifteen million human beings rather than three! (This was the opinion of Gustave de Beaumont, after Arthur Young.) As if the emigration of every healthy and industrious adult was not a nett loss for the country, just as is the guinea taken away by any *absentee !*

Is not his exit a sign of strength and energy in the emigrant? He was free to stay at home if he liked ; to shut himself up in a workhouse and live there at the public expense. Has he not given by his very departure the best proof that he is not a useless member in the social body? What! you incite all that is able and active to go away, keeping only the weak, the old, the useless ; to these you dole out what is necessary to keep up a flickering breath of life, and when poverty increases, you are surprised at it !

I bear in mind the reasons alleged by politicians. Elizabeth and Cromwell have invoked them before, when recurring to more drastic but equally vain measures. But, here again, the calculation is wrong ; the eternal justice of things has not permitted it to succeed.

For all those whom the feudal system starves out of their native island take care, for the most part, not to go and fertilize with their work the British colonies. Vainly does the emigration agent offer them a free passage, grants of land, and even premiums in money. They prefer buying with their last penny a ticket which opens a free land to them. They go to the United States, where they thrive almost to a miracle, and this is a decisive answer to the masters of their race, who are also its calumniators. They multiply there so as to form already a fifth part (twelve millions) of the total population of the great American Republic. At the bar, in the press, in all liberal professions, they are a majority, and by their brilliant qualities, which often secure them the first rank, they exercise a real preponderance. But they never forget that they are Irish. They keep the unimpaired remembrance of their beloved country, dear to their heart in proportion as she is unhappy. They remember their home burnt to the ground, the old grandfather thrown on the road-side, the little ones crying at the withered breast of a pallid mother, the wrench of parting, the heart-rending farewell; then the contumely during the voyage—the hardships after the landing; and they swear an oath that all shall be paid some day, and, in the meanwhile, they contribute their dollars to the healing of an ever-bleeding wound.

It is there that Fenianism was born. From their ranks come those conspirators who terrorize England with their periodic outrages. In all agrarian violence the hand of the emigrants is to be found. From 1848 to 1864 they have sent thirteen million pounds to those of their family that have remained in Ireland; and, from 1864 to 1887, perhaps double that sum. But in those figures, given by Lord Dufferin, the secret funds brought to the service of an ever-increasing agitation are not reckoned. The *Invincibles* were in their pay. The *Skirmishing Fund* was entirely sustained by them. The National League lives, in a manner, upon their subsidies. When Mr. Parnell went to visit the United States, they were powerful enough to induce the Senate of Washington to give him the honours of the sitting—an exception which stands unique in history.

The independence of Ireland is their dream, their ambition, their hope, their luxury in life. The day when this is accomplished, England will perhaps realize that the Irish emigration has been a political blunder, as it is an economical mistake and a moral crime.

CORK.

Wishing to see some of those who emigrate I have come to Cork. Cork is the great harbour of the South of Ireland, the gate that opens on America and Australia. From St. Patrick's Bridge on the Lee a steamer took me to where three emigrant ships were at anchor ready to fly to other climes. I went on board two of them, one English, the other American. There was nothing particular to notice, except an under-deck disposed as a dormitory, as is the rule on board all maritime transports, so as to lodge four or five hundred steerage passengers. These passengers bring with them their bedding, which consists generally of a coarse blanket, and the staple part of their eatables. A canteen affords them, at reasonable prices, all drinks or extras that they may think fit to add to their ordinary fare.

The impression I gather in these under-decks is rather a favourable one. There is as yet only the bare floor, but it is clean and well washed. Through the hatches, wide open, a pure and bracing air circulates freely.

No doubt there will be some alteration after a few days' voyage. But it is evident that the Queen's administration keeps a sharp eye upon the emigration companies, and sees that all sanitary prescriptions are observed. One sees no longer now-a-days such scandalous spectacles as occurred in the years of the famine, when thousands of Irish were promiscuously heaped in the hold of *coffin-ships*, and died by hundreds before reaching the goal. Emigration is now one of the normal, it may be said one of the official, functions of social life in Ireland—a function which has its organs, laws, customs, and even its record-office. The companies keep their agents in all British possessions; they are informed of all the wants of those colonies; they know what specialists are in demand, what advantages are offered to the new-comer. They do their best to make the offer fit with the demand, and they seem to succeed.

An old boatswain on board one of the emigrant ships tells me that life there is generally monotonous but quiet. The passengers do not mix or associate as quickly as one could imagine. Each of them pitches his own separate camp on the few square feet that chance gives him, and it is only after eight or ten days' voyage that they begin to club together. The mothers tend their babies, the fathers smoke their pipes, the children play, the young people flirt. It appears that a relatively considerable number of marriages are prepared and even concluded in the crossing. There is nothing surprising in that, if we remember that the most numerous class of emigrants is composed of marriageable girls and men between twenty and twenty-five years of age.

A few types of emigrants taken at the inns and public-houses on the quays. *John Moriarty*, of Ballinakilla, County Cork, 45 to 50 years old. A rural Micawber, dressed in a dilapidated black coat, a pair of green trousers, completely worn out at the knees, and crushed hat. A Catholic (he says *Cathioulic*). Squats with wife and children in a single room, almost devoid of furniture. Was to have embarked five days ago for Canada. The Board of Health did not allow it on account of one of the children having got the measles (an illness which assumes in Great Britain a most dangerous and infectious character). Makes no difficulty to tell me his whole history. Had a farm of thirteen acres. Was thriving more or less—rather less than more. But for the last seven years it has been an impossibility for him to make both ends meet.

Strange as it may appear, the man is a Conservative in feeling.

"Nothing to do in the country, with those *mob laws* and agitation!" says he.

"What mob laws?"

"Well, the trash on fixity of tenure, fair rent and the rest."

"I thought they were favourable to the tenant."

"Favourable in one sense, yes, sir," (*with a diplomatic air, as he fastens on me two little chocolate-coloured eyes*) "but disastrous in the end, because they allow one to sell his tenant-right at a discount. You believe that it will set you up, and it is the very stone that makes you sink. The banks are our ruin, don't you see? Once they have taken hold of their man they don't let him out before they have skinned him" (*a silence, then a sigh of mild envy*). "It is, indeed, a good trade that of banking!"

He remains dreamy and seems to meditate the scheme of founding a bank in Canada.

Martin Mac Crea, 22 years old, a shepherd of Drumcunning. A Catholic. A tall, pale, thin fellow, decently dressed, with a wide awake look. Goes to Queensland. Why? "Because there is no opening in Ireland. The most you can do is to earn your bare sustenance." It appears that in Queensland it is quite a different affair. The profession of shepherd pays there. Let a man bring or save the money necessary to buy half-a-dozen sheep, and let them graze at their will. Seven or eight years later their name is legion, and the man is rich.

' But are you then quite free of ties here? Don't you leave anybody, any relation, in Ireland?"

"I was obliged to live far from them, and where I go I shall be more able to help them. Besides, the post reaches there."

"And the young ladies at Drumcunning. Do they allow you to go away without a protest?"

A broad smile lights up Martin Mac Crea's countenance. A further conversation informs me that his betrothed has gone before him to Brisbane, where she is a servant. He is going to meet her, and they shall settle together in the *bush,* keeping sheep on their own account.

Let us hope she has waited for him. Queensland is far away!

Pat Coleman, twenty years old. A friend to the former. Son of a small farmer with six children. Nothing to do at home. Prefers going to the Antipodes, to see if there is a way there to avoid dying of starvation, as happened to his grandfather.

Peter Doyle, forty-three years old. A journeyman. A Presbyterian. Can't find work at home; therefore emigrates. Was employed on railway construction, county Clare. Has been turned away, the line being completed and open to travellers. Had come to Cork in the hope of getting work, but found only insignificant jobs. Packed to Melbourne.

Dennis O'Rourke, twenty-nine years old ; of Enniscorthy, Wexford. An engine-maker; belongs to a class of which I had as yet met no specimen in Ireland, the workman-politician. Has already emigrated to the United States, where he spent three years. Wished to see his country again, and tried to set up a business on a small scale, first in Dublin, then at Cork; but it does not pay. Goes back to New York.

"Do you know why? I am going to tell you. (*Fiercely*) I am going because this country is rotten to the core! Because it has no spirit left, not even that of rebellion! I am going because I will no longer bear on my back the weight of dukes and peers, of Queen, Prince of Wales, Royal family, and the whole lot of them! I am going where you can work and be free; where a man is worth another when he has got in his pocket two dollars honestly earned. That is where I go, and why I go."

"In short, you make England responsible for your misfortunes?"

"England be damned!"

It is O'Connell's word. He was travelling in

France, towards St. Omer, and found himself inside the mail-coach with an old officer of the first Empire who began forthwith to talk against the English. The great Irish agitator kept silent.

"Don't you hear me?" the other said at last, insolently.

"I beg your pardon, I hear you perfectly well."

"And you don't mind my treating your country as I do?"

"England is not my country; I hate it more than you will ever do."

CHAPTER XII.

THE LEACUE.

ENNIS.

THE county Clare, and more especially Ennis, its chief town, have played an important part in the contemporary history of Ireland. It was here eight years ago (in 1879) that Mr. Parnell, at a great autumn meeting, gave his famous *mot d'ordre* on social and political interdict.

"If you refuse to pay unjust rents, if you refuse to take farms from which others have been evicted, the land question must be settled, and settled in a way that will be satisfactory to you. Now, what are you to do to a tenant who bids for a farm from which another has been evicted? You must shun him on the roadside where you meet him,—you must shun him in the shops,—you must shun him in the fair green, and in the market-place, and in the place of worship: by leaving him severely alone, by putting him in a moral Coventry; by isolating him from the rest of his countrymen, as if he were the leper of old, you must show him your detestation of the crime he has committed."

Those words contained a whole programme, faithfully carried out since, and which has already borne fruit. They took exceptional force from the fact that Mr. Parnell, at the time he pronounced them, was already the acknowledged leader of Irish opposition. They were in some sort the registration of birth of the League.

The League! Every moment, travelling through this island, one comes in contact with this power, mysterious though positive, anonymous and yet implicitly recognized. The League houses and feeds evicted families; it settles that such a landlord or such a farmer shall be boycotted; it decrees that the rents of such an estate shall be reduced 30 per cent.; that of such another the rents shall be lodged in the League's own coffers; it patronises candidatures, chooses the place and time of meetings, presides over all the phases of social life. What is that League? is the question one asks.

At first one naturally supposes it to be an electoral association such as exists in every free country. But little by little one perceives that it is a far bigger affair. Electoral associations are not in the habit of inspiring such persistent enthusiasm, of covering during eight long years the extent of a whole country; they do not send roots to the most remote villages, nor do they count among their members three-quarters of the adult population. It is not their custom either to fulminate excommunications, or if they do they have but little appreciable effect on the ordinary tenour of life. One never heard that they disposed of important capital, and one would be less surprised to hear that they had entered into a lawsuit with their printer about an unpaid bill for five or six thousand placards, than one would be to hear that they have several hundred thousand pounds in the bank.

And yet it is precisely of hundred thousand pounds that one constantly hears in connection with the League. Where does it get all that money, in a country worn so threadbare as this? Whence is it that it is so universally respected, so religiously obeyed? All the smiles are for the League, while the functionaries of the Crown pocket only snubbings. All the doors open before the League, while they close and even barricade themselves at the bare mention of the Lord Lieutenant's name.

One observes these facts; compare and weigh them. Then the conclusion imposes itself quite naturally that the League is the only public power recognised by the bulk of the Irish nation. One already had a suspicion of being a spectator to a revolution, of which the violent deeds, instead of being concentrated over a period of two or three years, as we have seen at home, have spread over half a century. One understands that one has fallen in the midst of a civil war, not in the incipient state, but fully let loose, and that there exists in this island two rival authorities,—that of the Crown with the bayonets on its side; that of the League, possessing all hearts.

Ireland, it is hardly necessary to repeat, has been in a state of rebellion since the beginning of the British Conquest. But it has been in a state of revolution only for a period of about forty years. Insurrection betrayed itself now by individual but constant acts of rebellion, of which one can easily follow the succession through past ages, now by collective risings like those of Thomas Fitzgerald in 1534, of O'Neil in 1563, of Desmond in 1579, of Preston in 1642, of the Whiteboys in 1791, of the Oakboys in 1762, of the Steelboys in 1768, of Wolfe Tone in the course of the French Revolution, of Emmet in 1803, of the New Whiteboys in 1807, of John Mitchell in 1848, of the Fenians in 1865 and 1867. As for the agrarian revolution, born of an economical situation impossible to bear, it follows its course as regularly as a great river, ever getting larger and larger, widening its bed, swelling its volume with all the streams it meets, increasing in power at the same time that its waters get more depth and breadth. Even the soothing mixtures prescribed for it by the Parliamentary doctors have served as its tributaries. Its torrent has at length become irresistible.

To discover its source, we must go back to the famine evictions of 1847. The heart-rending spectacle then presented by Ireland made it natural to look for a palliation to such misery. The malady was studied in all its aspects; much learned discussion took place at the bedside of the agonizing patient. It was the time when Disraeli developed his famous theory of "the three profits." The land, if one was to believe him, must yield profit to three persons:—the Queen, the landlord, and the tenant. It appears this was arranged from the end of Time by the Great Architect of the Universe. The laws of Kepler are not more absolute. The unlucky thing is that the earth does not always fulfil its obligations, and too often refuses to yield up the three sacramental profits.

Theorists endowed with less boldness thought to find a remedy by giving legal consecration to the tenant's rights by the system of *the three F's*, as it was called, that is to say, *Fair Rent, Fixity of Tenure, and Free Sale*. Through endless resistance, after endless debating in the course of twenty parliamentary sessions, a whole *remedial* legislation came to add its bulk to the already so intricate structure of Anglo-Saxon law.

Now the custom of Ulster was extended to the whole of Ireland, and the right of the farmer over the improvements paid with his money became law (1860); now he was promised an indemnity in case of eviction, and the basis was laid of a system of amortization which must infallibly in the course of time have ended in creating a class of peasant landowners (1870).

Already in the year 1849, the State had interfered between the landlords in difficulties and their tenants, by the creation of a special tribunal for obligatory liquidation,—*the Encumbered Estates Court*. It finally came to interfere between landlord and tenant by instituting a new court of arbitration, the *Land Court*, entrusted with the care of fixing the "fair" rent in each case.

That Court was no sooner opened than 75,807 affairs were inscribed upon its roll. It judged in one year 15,676. But there remained still 60,101 to be judged, and already the reductions of 18 to 27 per cent. imposed on the landlords appeared insufficient; already the farmers were loudly clamouring for further reductions.

For in truth such remedies were too anodine for such rooted disease! But the wedge had nevertheless entered the tree. The State had appeared in the character of umpire between the landlord and the peasant. Henceforth all was or seemed possible.

The essence of dogmas is to suffer no questioning. One cannot with impunity discuss for twenty years the basis of landed property's law and the theory of " the three profits " before empty stomachs. As a parallel to these debates, the question of political rights for Ireland rose again, and ended insensibly by the conquest of the electoral franchise, of religious equality, and of national education. The moment arrived when the bulk of the population took an interest only in the truly vital question,—that of the soil. And all of a sudden they understood that there was only one remedy for the ills that weighed so grievously over them: Landlords and tenants cannot continue to live side by side. Either the one or the other must go.

" Let the landlords decamp! They do not belong here," said the peasants.

"No, by G——! The peasants shall go," answered the landlords; "the way is open . . . ."

It was thus that towards 1876 the Irish movement became agrarian, from being purely national. The League is the organ of that new function.

Its primary idea belongs to two veterans of the Fenian plots, Michael Davitt and John Devoy. But what distinguishes it from those plots, besides a broader basis and larger aims, is that it acts in broad daylight, with face uncovered, appealing to all men of goodwill, using exclusively those constitutional weapons—the right of meeting, the right of association and coalition.

"The Fenians saw only the green flag," wrote John Devoy. "The men of to-day perceive that under its folds is the Irish land." Nevertheless, it was to the remains of the Fenian associations that he and Michael Davitt had recourse at first to lay the foundations of the new association. They went to look for them even to the uttermost end of America, secured the co-operation of some of the most influential members of the Irish emigration, then came back to Europe, and summoned a great preliminary meeting at Irishtown.

As ordinarily enough happens in such cases, their project was at first looked upon coldly by members of Parliament, who thought it impolitic, and violently opposed by the secret societies—Fenians or Ribbonmen—who thought it calculated to cool the Nationalist zeal. But under the too real sufferings produced by two years of famine (1876—1877), the agrarian tempest assumed such formidable proportions, that all resistance had to cease, and the politicians were compelled to lower their flag. For the chiefs of the autonomist party it was a question of no less than keeping or losing their mandate. Either they would adopt the new evangel, or they would be left lying, officers without troops, on the electoral battle-field. Most of them understood this in time.

Mr. Parnell, the most conspicuous of all, had till then limited his part to the demand for a national government for Ireland, and his tactics to parliamentary obstruction. From an economical point of view he still remained, with all his party, on the level of worthy Mr. Butt's *three F's*. He was one of the first to understand that it was all over with Home Rule, and with his own political fortune, if he hesitated any longer to plunge into deeper waters.

He made his plunge with characteristic resolution. "There is no longer any possibility of conciliation between landlord and tenant," he said. "Since the one or the other must go out, it is better that the less numerous class should be the one to do it." On the 8th of June, 1879, at Westport, he pronounced his famous, " Keep a firm grip on your homesteads!" From the 21st of October following the agrarian League promulgated circulars, which he signed as president.

The League's aim and watchword were—*The land for the peasant!* Its means were the union of all the rural forces, the formation of a resistance fund for evicted farmers, the strike of tenants with a view to compelling the landlords to grant a reduction of rent; and incessant agitation in favour of a law for the liquidation of landed property, which would give the land into the hands of the cultivators by means of partial payments made during a certain number of years.

The success of such a programme, seconded by the political leaders of Ireland, was certain. But its promoters never had dared to hope for a rush such as was experienced in a few weeks' time. Adhesions poured in by thousands; all the social classes embraced it. The Catholic clergy themselves, after wavering one moment, found it advisable to follow in the footsteps of the revolutionary party, as the Deputies had done before them. Everywhere local boards were formed which put themselves at the disposal of the central committee. Almost everywhere the Catholic priest, his curates, not unfrequently the Anglican priest himself, were found among the members of the board.

This is enough to show with what alacrity and unanimity the mobilisation of the agrarian army was effected. Far from weakening the Nationalist party, as was feared by its prebendaries, it came out of this tempered afresh, enlarged, associated with the everyday interests, tied indissolubly henceforth, for the majority of an agricultural population, to the most secret if the most ardent wish of their labourers' heart.

What remained to do was to endow the League with the resources wanted to carry out its programme; but it was not in a country practically ruined, a prey to the tortures of hunger, literally reduced to beggary, that those resources were to be found. Mr. Parnell set out for the land of dollars. He preached the new word there with complete success. Exotic branches of the League were established in the various States of America, in Canada, and Australia; the only thing remaining to do was to organize the *in partibus infidelium* government that was to take in hand the direction of Ireland.

But a short time since this government sat in a palace of the finest street in Dublin—Sackville Street. There it had its offices, reception rooms, council-room furnished with the orthodox green baize table, its ministerial departments, secretaries and writers, officially headed paper, its stamp, documents, accounts and red tape.

After a recent movement on the offensive on the part of the enemy, the League had to decamp and put all this material in a place of safety. But though it be presently without a known place of abode, the League none the less pursues its work. Do not telegraphic wires keep it in communication with its agents throughout the length and breadth of the territory? Why were Transatlantic cables invented, if not for the purpose of opening permanent communications between the League and its American, Australian, and Asiatic colonies? In all the extent of its jurisdiction, which is that of the globe, the League is obeyed and respected; it possesses the confidence of its innumerable tributaries.

Perhaps that comes from the fact that this committee, though it sometimes accented too much the professional character of its members, has at least the rare merit of faithfully serving its constituents and of being in perfect harmony of conscience with them.

Perhaps this is due to the effect of direct subsidies; and we must see there something better than a mere coincidence,—a great lesson for the democracies of the future. One thing is certain: this government, after wielding power for eight years, have their party well in hand. They are able to do without red tape or scribbling. One word is enough to indicate their will, and if they lack secretaries, a hundred newspapers will carry this word to its address.

It would be a matter of some difficulty to appreciate rightly the financial resources of the League Competent judges estimate them at an income of two million francs. It receives on an average, from English-speaking countries, a thousand pounds a week. Now and then subscriptions slacken, and the incoming of money is smaller; but the least incident, such as a noisy arrest or a political law-suit, is sufficient to awaken the zeal of the leaguers. That zeal is always proportionate to the energy of resistance opposed by the Cabinet of St. James to the government of Sackville Street. If London so much as raises its head, at once Dublin, and behind Dublin the whole of Ireland, the whole of Irish America, Australia, the Cape, and the extreme depths of India, all are shaken to their very centre,—in other words, they pay.

The chief treasurer of the League, Mr. Egan, giving account of his administration in October, 1882, after a space of three years, stated that during these three years £244,820 had passed through his hands. In this total one-third only came from insular contributors; all the rest came from abroad. £50,000 had been given in relief of distress; over £15,000 had been spent in State trials; nearly £148,000 had been expended through the general Land League and the Ladies' Land League in support of evicted tenants, providing wooden houses, law costs, sheriffs' sales, defence against ejectments and various local law proceedings, and upon the general expenses of the organization. A little over £31,900 remained to the account of the association.

There are no reasons for supposing the normal receipts of the League to have diminished much since that period. More recently (in 1886) the "plan of campaign" has created new openings for it.

This "plan of campaign," one of the boldest conceptions ever accepted by a great political party, consists simply in lodging into the coffers of the League, and for its use, the rents that were pronounced excessive by its committee, and that the landlords refused to abate. Let us mention in passing that the Catholic Archbishop of Dublin publicly accepted the responsibility of this tremendous war-measure. It has, we must add, been exercised with obvious moderation, in specific cases only, and by way of example. The true weapon of the League, that which it used most liberally up to the present day, is the *boycotting*, or social interdict pitilessly pronounced against any one who disobeys its behests.

From a legal point of view, the League has met with various fortunes. Suppressed in 1881 by an Act of Parliament, it was compelled to put on a mask and to disguise itself under the name of the *Ladies' League*. A year later it underwent a new incarnation and became the *National League*.

Now the Tory Ministry has suppressed it once more *proclaimed* it, as they say (*clameur de haro*), in virtue of the special power conferred on it. It appears improbable that the health of the association should suffer much for this; on the contrary, it will probably be all the better for it. In former days it would have been content to undergo a fourth avatar by taking the name of *Celtic League, Irish Babies' League*, or any other name that would have done just as well to deride its adversaries. A special provision of the Coercion Act will prevent its having recourse to this expedient. By the 7th article of the Act, the Lord Lieutenant is empowered to suppress any *new* association formed with a view to continuing the affairs of the old ones.

But one never thinks of everything. Precisely because it is so explicit, the 7th article cannot apply to the *old* Irish societies, different from the National League, and which can easily be substituted in its place. Those associations, *Home Rule Unions, Liberal Federations*, &c., are numerous through the country. One of them could easily accept the inheritance of the League, and it would be necessary to convoke Parliament to suppress it. If Parliament suppresses it, it will be easy to find something else. And so on for ever, through ages, to the crack of doom. . . . In the meanwhile there will be protestations, agitations, interpellations, and before the end, "the King, the ass" . . . or the Ministry shall have died, as La Fontaine said.

Lord Salisbury may close two hundred offices of the League in the counties of Clare and Kerry. How shall he close the offices beyond the sea, which are the real ones?

In fact, the League is indestructible, because it is

impossible to get hold of it. One can arrest its chiefs, as has been done often enough, intercept its correspondence, oppose cavalry regiments to its public demonstrations, and retroactive measures to its secret acts ; they cannot destroy the faith the Irish people have put in it ; they cannot grapple with the essence of an association which rests on the most vital interests of the peasantry.

Political persecution is fatally doomed to failure when exercised in a free country, if it does not begin by attacking the press and the right of meeting. And who shall dare to touch those two pillars of the British edifice ? The English government is the government of opinion, or it is nothing : now, the opinion of the majority of Irishmen, of the majority of Scotchmen, and of an imposing minority of Englishmen, is in favour of the League.

To say the truth, all parties are agreed *in petto* upon the necessity of abolishing landlordism. It is only a question of settling who shall have the credit of doing it, and how it shall be managed so that neither the landlord's creditors nor the public exchequer should suffer too much by that unavoidable liquidation. Therefore all the measures taken against an organism that incarnates such general feeling can only be an empty fooling, a holiday sport. Their only effect must be to awaken rural passions and provoke new acts of violence. One might even believe such was their only aim. For, to be able to ruin a perfectly lawful association like the League, in a country of free discussion, it is indispensable first to throw dishonour upon it.

They have not yet succeeded in doing this, in spite of the most strenuous efforts. Not only has it always been impossible to charge the League with any act contrary to the current standard of morals, but it is beyond any doubt that its influence is especially directed towards the prevention of agrarian crimes, and even against individual resistance to landlordism. Wherever there is popular emotion or possible disorder, its delegates are present, and endeavour to enforce respect for the law. If it happen that the orations of some underlings overstep the mark, the general methods of the League none the less remain unimpeachable. It has taken for mandate the ruling of revolutionary action, the legalizing it, the task of giving it a scientific character. It is to its honour that it has succeeded up to the present day. One may reasonably suppose that it will not change its tactics at the hour when its true chief is no longer Mr. Parnell, but practically Mr. Gladstone.

CHAPTER XIII.

THE CLERGY.

From Kilrush, on the coast of Clare, an excellent service of steamers goes up the estuary of the Shannon to Foynes, where one takes the train to Limerick. It is a charming excursion, undertaken by all tourists. The Shannon here is of great breadth and majesty, flowing in an immense sheet of water, recalling the aspect of the great rivers of America. At the back you have the stormy ocean; in front, on the right, on the left, green hills dotted with snowy villas. Few trees or none, as is the rule in Ireland, but a light haze that softens all the outlines of the ground, magnifies the least shrubs, and lends to all the view a melting aspect of striking loveliness.

The boats are few in number, though the depth of the channel would allow ships of the heaviest tonnage to go up to within five miles of Limerick. I notice hardly two or three sailing boats at anchor on this four hours' journey. What an admirable harbour for an active commerce would be that broad estuary, opening directly opposite to America, on the extreme point of the European continent. It is the natural point of arrival and departure for the Transatlantic steamers, which would reach New York in five days from there. Engineers have dreamed of this possibility. But to justify a maritime movement, and legitimise such enterprise, a great commerce, an industry that Ireland lacks, would be wanted. Gentlemen of an engineering turn, come back again in a century or two.

At Tarbert, where we stop to take passengers, a fort opens its loop-holes, armed with guns, on the river. Redcoats are encamping at the foot of the fortress, and the morning breeze carries to us the rough voice of a non-commissioned officer drilling his men. One might imagine him addressing the *Invincibles* across the ocean somewhat after this guise:

"Here we are, keeping watch: If ever this alluring bay tempt you to come over, you shall find us ready to receive you!" . . . .

The helm trembles; the boat goes on its course, and soon Tarbert melts behind us in the sunny haze.

On board, the travellers resemble those seen in

summer on all great rivers—merchants bent on a pleasure trip; judges and barristers, having taken leave of briefs; professors enjoying their holidays, with wives, daughters, sons, goods, and chattels—all have the sun-burnt complexion and the satisfied look one brings back from the seaside. They have been staying on the beautiful shores of the County Clare, and are returning home with a provision of health for one year. La Fontaine has already noticed that, travelling, one is sure to see "the monk poring over his breviary." Here the proportion is far greater than in the ancient coach; it is not one priest we have on board, but a dozen, all sleek, fat, and prosperous, dressed in good stout broadcloth, as smooth as their rubicund faces, and provided with gold chains resting on comfortable abdomens.

One remark, by the way. When you meet an Irish peasant on the road, he stops, wishes you good-day, and adds, "Please, sir, what is the time?" Not that he cares much to know. He is perfectly well able to read the time on the great clock of the heavens. But it is his own manner of saying, "I can see, sir, that you are a man of substance—one of the great ones of this earth—*since you have a watch.* My sincere congratulations!"

Well, all those travelling priests possess chronometers—we are obliged to notice it, since it appears to be a sign of easy circumstances in Ireland—and the rest of their attire fully carries out that symptom. Under the undefinable cut that at once betrays a clerical garment, their black coat has all the softness of first quality cloth; their travelling bag is of good bright leather; their very umbrella has a look of smartness, and does not affect the lamentable droop that with us is always associated with the idea of a clerical umbrella. Some of them wear the Roman hat and collar, with a square-cut waistcoat and the ordinary trousers of the laity, and stockings of all the hues of the rainbow. A young curate sports violet-coloured ones, which he exhibits with some complacency. I ventured to ask him, in the course of conversation, whether he belonged to the Pope's household. He answered with a blush of modesty that he had not that honour, and wore violet hose because he was fond of that colour.

That is a matter of taste; but I have a right to suppose, young Levite, that the mitre and episcopal rochet—perhaps even the cardinal purple—hover at night over your ingenuous dreams.

LIMERICK.

Limerick is a big town of 40,000 inhabitants, celebrated for its hams, lace, and gloves. The objects of interest are an important linen factory, and another for military equipments, besides a stone mounted on a pedestal, and which served as a table for signing the famous treaty of 1691—soon violated like all treaties, however. Opposite that historic stone, on the other side of the Shannon, the ancient castle of King John rears its proud head; it has a grim and gloomy look, with its seven towers, its thick walls and iron-bound gates.

At the large hotel of the place I meet again three of my ecclesiastical fellow-travellers. They evidently know what is good for them, and would on no account stop at second-rate inns. One cannot blame them for it. But this is a sign of prosperity, added to all the others; a hotel at fifteen shillings a day, without counting the wine, seems at first sight suited to prelates rather than to humble clergymen. Yet these are only village and parish priests, as I gather from the book on which I sign my name after theirs. At dinner, where we sit side by side, I am compelled to see that the appetite of the reverend fathers is excellent, and that the *carte* of the wines is a familiar object with them. They each have their favourite claret : one likes Léoville, another Château Margaux, while the third prefers Chambertin ; and they drain the cup to the last drop. After dessert they remain last in the dining-room, in company with a bottle of port.

At ten o'clock that night, entering it to get a cup of tea, I find the three seated round glasses of smoking toddy.

These memorable events are not consigned here, it need hardly be said, for the vain satisfaction of recording that on a certain evening three Irish priests were tippling freely. They certainly had a perfect right to do so, if such was their bent. It is the most cherished privilege of a British subject; and of all capital sins proscribed by the Church, drunkenness is certainly the most innocent. But this remark, made without prejudice, during a chance meeting at an inn, carries out the general impression left by the Irish clergy—that of a corporation greatly enamoured of its comforts, endowed with good incomes, and whose sleekness forms a striking contrast with the general emaciation of their parishioners.

Everywhere, in visiting this island, one meets with this typical pair of abbots, well dressed and well "groomed," travelling comfortably together, and, to use a popular expression, "la coulant douce." It is startling in this realm of poverty, the more startling because the Catholic clergy have no official means of existence, no salary paid them by the State. They owe all the money they spend to the private contributions of their admirers. Was there ever, they doubtlessly think, a more legitimate way of making money? That is probably why they make so little mystery of it, and disdain to hide when they exchange part of their income against a bottle of Chambertin. In other places, priests think that a certain reserve is expected of them; they prefer being securely shut in privacy before they carve a partridge or plentifully moisten a synod dinner. Here they are so secure in their position that they recoil from no profane glance.

Their lives are, I am told, of exemplary purity. I have no difficulty in believing it, both because purity is a marked characteristic of the race, and because their faith has seemed to me simple as that of the Breton priests. There must be exceptions, and some were pointed out to me; but assuredly those exceptions are few in number. By many signs which do not deceive those who have some experience of life, one can see that the Irish priest has not the vices of the Italian or Spanish priest. He is a gormandizer, to be sure, but he is chaste—perhaps for the very reason that he is so devoted to the pleasures of the table. His simplicity of heart is wonderful sometimes, and makes one think of those Mount Athos monks, nursed in the cloister from the tenderest age, and who know literally nothing of the exterior world. I heard two of them, old men both, who were quietly chatting in a corner of the railway carriage. Both had small, bald birds' heads, shaven chins, and a quaint, old-fashioned look.

"*I am next door to an idiot!*" one of them was saying, with curious complacency.

"So am I," answered the other; "so was I always, and I thank Almighty God for it! . . . . . for have you not noticed that all those grand, clever people often lose the faith? . . . . ."

Where does their income come from? That is a question doubly interesting to us Frenchmen, who every year pay out two million sterling for the budget of public worship. A placard seen everywhere in Limerick, and presenting a marked resemblance to the advertisement for a theatre, will help to tell us. This placard is to the effect that on the day after tomorrow a general ordination of young priests will take place in the Cathedral of St. John, by the hands of the Right Reverend X. O'Dyer, archbishop of the town (the name and quality in conspicuous characters), assisted by several other prelates and dignitaries. It proceeds to state that excursion trains have been established for the occasion, and that tickets for the ceremony may be procured, at the price of half-a-crown and one shilling, at No. 98, George Street.

This is a booking-office, exactly like those we have in theatres. Plenty of placards, the plan of the church showing the number and position of each seat, a table of prices, and behind a little grated window a bearded old woman for the tickets,—nothing is wanting. One has only to choose one's place, to pay the price down, and to take away the ticket. About twenty persons perform these various acts before my eyes. Evidently the receipt will be good. The cathedral of St. John, that proudly raises its brand-new spire above all the others, must be able to accommodate at least three or four thousand spectators. At 1*s.* 9*d.* per head on an average, that gives already a total of two or three hundred pounds. To this must be added the product of the collections and that of the wooden money-boxes, that open everywhere to receive the outcome of the generosity of the faithful; the total, we may be sure, cannot be otherwise than respectable. It is true that an ordination is not an every-day event, and that it must be an expensive affair to put on the stage. We must therefore suppose the ordinary income to be raised by way of semestrial and direct contribution.

This is how the thing is done: each parish priest has two Sundays in the year devoted to the taking his *dues*, as he calls it. On these days, instead of preaching, he exhibits a manuscript list upon which are inscribed by name all his tributaries, that is to say, all his parishioners, with the sums they have paid into his hands; this he reads publicly. As a rule he adds a running commentary to each name, either to praise the generosity of the donor, or, on the contrary, to complain of his stinginess. In the country, especially, the scene is not wanting in humour.

"*Daniel MacCarthy*, four shillings and six-pence," says the priest. "That's not much for a farmer who keeps three cows and sold two calves this year. I will hope for him that he only meant that as a preliminary gift. . . . *Simon Redmond*, seven shillings and six-pence; he might have given ten shillings, as he did last year. He is not what we should call a progressive man. . . . *George Roehe*, two shillings and three-pence. *Richard MacKenna*, one shilling and three-pence. *Denis Twoney*, one shilling and nine-pence. Against those who do their best I have nothing to say. *Michael Murphy*, fifteen shillings. Now, I ask, could not he have made it a pound? The pity of it! *John Coleman*, five shillings. *Daniel Clune*, five shillings. *Cornelius Nagle*, five shillings. One would think they had agreed to do it. . . . . *Henry Townsend*, Esq., of Townsend Manor, three pounds sterling. That's what I call a subscriber! And he is a Protestant. You ought to be ashamed of yourselves to let a Protestant be more generous to your own church than you are. . . . *Harriet O'Connor*, one shilling and nine-pence. I will be bound she liked buying a new bonnet better than doing her duty. That is between her and her conscience. But I am afraid that at the Day of Judgment she won't find it such a good investment. . . . *Mary Ann Cunningham*, twelve shillings and nine-pence. If everybody knew how to spare and how to use what they spare in the same way as this good lady, things would go better in this world and in the next, take my word for it. . . . *Colonel Lewis*, of Knockamore Villa, five pounds sterling. Another Protestant! Positively one might think one lived in a parish of heathens when one sees that the heretics alone seem to have some regard for the church! . . ."

The reading goes on in this guise, adorned with reflections more or less pungent, and interrupted now and then by a repartee coming from the far end of the audience, and torn from the patient by the malignity of the attack; a general hilarity is then provoked without impairing in the least the reverence of the congregation for their priest or their church. This semestrial subscription, added to the weekly collections, the daily masses, the baptisms, weddings and burials, is amply sufficient to keep the church, the priest, and the priest's house in a good state of repair. Most of the parish priests besides, have the habit of " binage," that is to say they often say two or three masses a day, at different points of their sometimes very wide parish.

They are generally addressed by their christian name, prefaced by the name of *Father: Father James*, *Father Henry*, etc., and this title well describes the terms of filial familiarity of the flocks with their pastor,—a familiarity not unfrequently manifested by sound boxes on the ear for children, and good blows with the stick on the shoulders of his grown-up parishioners, but which does not preclude respect. In the streets one always sees the parish priest respectfully greeted by the passers by; many women kneel down to kiss his hand as in Italy or Spain.

His authority is that of a patriarch, who not only wields spiritual power, but also, to a great extent, social and political power. He incarnates at once in himself the native faith so long proscribed in the country, resistance to the oppressor, heavenly hopes and compensation for human trials. As a consequence, his influence is great, for good as for ill.

The faith of the Irish peasant is entire, unquestioning, absolute as that of a thirteenth century's serf. One must see on Sundays those churches crowded to overflowing, and too narrow for the congregation who remain, silent and kneeling, on the steps and even outside the doors. One must see those ragged people, forming a chain by holding on to each other's tatters, one behind the other, at a distance of 50 to 60 feet from the altar, a patch of dim light up there in the darkness of the church; or else they must be seen at some pilgrimage round a miraculous well or stream, like the Lough Derg, wallowing indiscriminately in the pond, washing therein their moral and physical uncleanliness, drinking the sacred water by the pailful, intoxicated with enthusiasm and hope.

The devotees of Our Lady del Pilar, and of San

Gennaro, are less expansive and less ardent. The Sacred Heart of Jesus, the Rosary, St. Philip of Neri, all the mystical armoury of the modern church have innumerable votaries in Ireland. One would perhaps experience some difficulty in finding there ten born Catholics not wearing next to their skin some amulet made of cloth or ivory, and invested in their eyes with supernatural powers. If I do not greatly err, St. Peter's pence must find its more generous contributors amidst those poverty-stricken populations. To those imaginations of starved and half hysterical people the Roman pontiff appears in the far distance, all in white, in a halo of gold, like a superhuman vision of Justice and Pity in this world where they found neither the one nor the other.

An Irish servant in London once asked my advice about the investment of her savings, some thirty pounds which she had scraped together at the Post Office Savings Bank. I congratulated her on her thrift, when the poor girl told me, her eyes bright with unshed tears:

"It is for our Holy Father, that they keep in prison up there in Rome. . . . I mean to bring him fifty pounds as soon as ever I get them."

Those things may tend to explain why the only prosperous trade in Ireland is the clerical trade. Every year the number of priests increases, though the population is decreasing. In 1871 they numbered 3,136; in 1881 they were 3,363, or an increase of 227, under the guidance of four archbishops and twenty-four bishops. The Catholic population is of three million persons; that gives one priest for about 900 inhabitants.

It is generally admitted that each of these priests, with his church and his house, cannot cost much under £300 or £400 a year. That would give about £1,200,000 coming annually from the pockets of those labourers and servant girls. The tithe was never so heavy.

This clergy is chiefly recruited from the class of small farmers and peasantry (by the reason that the other classes are for the majority Protestants); as a consequence the clergy share all the passions of their class. The agrarian revolution has no agents more active. Almost everywhere the parish priest is the president of the local Land League Board. In the stormiest meetings is always to be found a village Peter the Hermit, preaching the new crusade and denouncing the landlords with fiery eloquence; not to speak of the Sunday preaching, which is only another meeting closed against the police, and where landlords are handled with extraordinary freedom of language. One has seen Irish priests openly declare a shot to be an unimportant trifle, so long as it was sent after a landed proprietor. A few months ago a Dublin paper mentioned a parish in Donegal, where the priest, they asserted, had gone so far as to put the properties of the landlords in lottery, by tickets of ten shillings each. The verification of this fact would by no means be easy. But, given the state of mind of the Irish priest, the ardour he brings into the struggle, the boundless indulgence he displays towards agrarian outrages, the tale is by no means improbable; our Leaguers have done even worse. However surprising may be in our Continental eyes the spectacle of a whole clergy taking part against the lords in a social war, under the paternal eyes of their episcopate, we must remember that here everything tends to bring about this result:—religious passions, hereditary instinct, and personal interest.

A priest who had the unlucky idea of pronouncing himself against the League would soon see his subsidies stopped. His flock would besides lose all confidence in him, and all respect for his person. I am told of a characteristic example of the kind of practical jokes indulged in such a case by the peasantry against the dissident pastor. A priest of the county Clare, seized by sudden scruples, took it into his head to abuse the League at the Sunday preaching, instead of sounding the usual praise in its honour. At once they sent him from the lower end of the church an old woman who begged to be heard directly in confession, before she could approach Holy Communion. The worthy man, grumbling a little at such an untimely fit of devotion, nevertheless acceded to her request with antique simplicity, and seated himself inside the confessional.

"Father," said the old woman in a loud voice, "I accuse myself of having this moment thought that you were a wicked bad man, who betrays his flock to take the part of their natural enemies. . . ."

"Amen!" answered all the congregation in a chorus.

Without waiting for absolution the old woman had got up to go. The priest tried to imitate her. Impossible. They had placed on his seat a huge lump of pitch which glued him, attached him indissolubly to his place. To get him free they were obliged to go for help outside, to call strangers to the rescue. The whole village meanwhile were shaking with laughter, and thought the joke in the best possible taste.

The Irish clergy go with the League, both because their temperament inclines them that way, and also because it is an imperious necessity of their situation ; their case is rather similar to that of the *Home Rule* members, who were compelled to enter the movement, whether they approved of it or not. However strong their hold on the mass of the rural population, their influence would vanish in a week if they tried to pull against the irresistible stream. Such sacrifices have never been a habit of the Roman Church.

Indeed it is permitted to smile, when one sees the Tory Ministry soliciting the intervention of the Pope in the Irish crisis, and obtaining from him the sending of a special legate entrusted with the mission of bringing the Episcopate of Ireland back to less subversive ideas. It is well understood that the Pope of course sends his legate, and derives from his diplomatic compliance all the advantages it entails. But he is better aware than any one that unless he personally gave away one million sterling a year to the parish priests of Ireland, he would have little reasonable hope of success in asking them to shift their policy.

Is it necessary to add that the Irish priest himself knows on occasion how to bring into his mundane relations the traditional suppleness and prudence of his order? A priest of Wexford, actively mixed up with the agrarian movement, was dining a few years ago at the house of Mr. C——, proprietor of a large landed estate in the county. Conversation turned upon the League, and no good was said of it. The priest listened in silence, without giving his sentiment either for or against the League. All of a sudden, with a look of assumed simplicity, he turned to his host—

"Look here, Mr. C——," he said, "Will you believe me? *Me impresshun is that there is no Land League.*"

The saintly man had for the last three months been vice-president of the board of the Land League in his district.

CHAPTER XIV.

FORT SAUNDERS.
Galway.

Galway is an old Spanish colony, planted on the western coast of Ireland, and which kept for a long time intimate relations with the mother country. Things and people have retained the original stamp to an uncommon degree ; but for the Irish names that are to be read on every shop, you could believe yourself in some ancient quarter of Seville. The women have the olive complexion, black hair, and red petticoat of the *mañolas;* the houses open on a courtyard, a thing unknown in other parts of Ireland, as well as in Great Britain ; they have grated windows, peepholes in the door, and are adorned with sculptures, in the Moorish style ; the steeples of churches affect the shape of minarets ; the very fishermen in the port, with the peculiar shape of their boat, sails and nets, and something indescribable in their general outline, remind you of the hardy sailors of Corunna.

The remembrance of seven or eight centuries of

busy trade with the Peninsula, does not show itself solely in faces, manners, or dwelling, it is to be found also in local tradition. Among others, there is the story of the Mayor Lynch Fitz-Stephen, who gave in 1493 such a fearful example of ruthless justice. His only son, whom he had sent to Spain to settle some important affair, was coming back with the Spanish correspondent of the family, bringing home a rich cargo, when he entered into a conspiracy with the crew, appropriated the merchandise, and threw overboard the unfortunate Spaniard. The crime was discovered, the culprit arrested, and brought to trial before his own father, who was exercising the right of high and low justice in the district, and by him condemned to the pain of death. The general belief was that the Mayor would contrive to find some pretext to give his son a respite; and in order to supply him with that pretext, his relations drew up a petition of grace, which they presented to him, covered with signatures. Lynch listened to their request, then merely told them to come back for an answer on a certain day he named. At the appointed time the suppliants appeared again; but the first sight which caught their eyes was the dead body of the Mayor's son hanging from one of the grated windows of his house. An inscription, placed in 1524, on the walls of the cemetery of St. Nicholas, records the memory of that event.

Galway is only a big borough nowadays, where ruins are nearly as numerous as inhabited dwellings. From the road that skirts the Bay, after leaving the harbour, the long islands of Arran may be seen rising on the west; from another road, which goes northwards, Lough Corrib appears, famous for its salmon fisheries. As an historic place, the county possessed already the field of Aughrim, celebrated for two centuries as the spot where James II. lost his last battle against William III.—a battle so murderous that the dogs of the country retained a taste for human flesh for three generations after. But since the last year it has acquired a new celebrity: another and no less epic battle has been fought at Woodford in August, 1886, for the agrarian cause. The account of it is worth telling. Never did the character of the struggle between League and landlord appear in such a glaring light. All the factors in the problem are there, each playing its own part. It is like a vertical cut opening Irish society down to its very core, and permitting to see it from basis to summit; a supplementary chapter to Balzac's *Paysans*.

Woodford is a pretty village seated on the shore of Lough Derg on the slope of the hills which divide

Galway from Clare. The principal landowners there are the Marquis of Clanricarde, Sir Henry Burke, the Westmeath family, Colonel Daly, and Lord Dunsandle. Agrarian hatred is particularly alive in that district; the Galway man is bloodthirsty, and counts human life as nought. Five or six years ago Mr. Blake, Lord Clanricarde's agent, was shot dead, and in March, 1886, a bailiff named Finley, a veteran of the Crimean war, had the same fate while he was going to proceed to an eviction on the account of Sir Henry Burke. The spot is shown still where the unfortunate man was murdered and his corpse left twenty-four hours without sepulture, nobody daring or willing to bear it away. A detachment of the police in the pay of the Property Defence Association having settled their barracks in the vicinity of Woodford, the inhabitants, about one thousand in number, organized a sort of grotesque pageant, which made its progress along the streets of the town behind a coffin bearing the inscription: *Down with landlordism!* then concluded by burning the coffin in sight of the barracks.

There are two churches, one Protestant, the other Catholic. The faithful who attend the first are two in number, no more nor less, which would be sufficient to show how legitimate it was for the Irish to protest when obliged to pay the tithes of an altogether alien worship. The second is headed by a jolly compeer, much beloved by his parishioners for his good humour and liberality, Father Caen, a pastor of the old school, whose boast it is that he keeps the best table and cellar, and has the prettiest nieces in the county. He is president of the local board of the League; the treasurer of that committee is the *guardian of the poor law* of the district, what we would call "l'administrateur du bien des pauvres;" but the true agent of the League—the *Deus ex machina* of the place—is the secretary, Father Egan, curate of the parish, an austere, thin, fanatic-looking man, a peasant's son, with all the passions of his race, who sucked the hatred of landlords with his mother's milk, and ever remembers that many of his kindred have been reduced to emigrate, and that an uncle of his went mad after being evicted. A feature to be noted down: that priest, tall, strong, sinewy, is an excellent shot and an inveterate poacher. Nothing would be easier for him than obtaining leave from the landowners to shoot on their grounds; but he scorns the leave. His delight is to lurk at night till he has shot some of their big game, or to head openly a *battue* for a general slaughter five miles round.

Fort Saunders.

One of the finest estates in the county is that of Lord Clanricarde, to which are attached three hundred and sixteen tenants.

Hubert George De Burgh Canning, Marquis of Clanricarde and Baron Somerhill, was born 1832, according to the *Peerage*. He was never married, has no children, belongs to the House of Lords as Baron Somerhill, is a member of two or three great clubs, and lives in Piccadilly, at the Albany, a sort of caravanserai (not to say seraglio), almost exclusively a resort of rich bachelors. That is about all that is known of him. His tenants do not know him. The only glimpse they ever had of their landlord was on the following occasion. In 1874, at the funeral of the late Marquis, a man of about forty, with fair hair, who had come from London for the ceremony, was noticed among the mourners. He was said to be the new master. That was all: he disappeared as he had come. Save for that hazy and far-away remembrance, the landlord is for the Woodford people a mere name, a philosophical entity of whom they know nothing except that he has a land agent at Loughrea, a little neighbouring town, and that into the hands of that agent they must pay every year £19,634 out of the product of the land. The tenants of Woodford are in that sum for about £1,000.

The Marquis's father died in 1874. Quite contrary to the present owner, he was the prototype of the Irish lord resident. Great sportsman, scatter-brain, violent, extravagant, but kind and open-handed, he was liked in spite of his numerous failings, and tradition helping him he was emphatically the master almost all his life long; a fact which he was wont to illustrate by boasting that if it pleased him to send his old grey mare to the House of Commons, the electors would be too happy to vote unanimously for the animal.

In 1872, however, the Marquis's tenants took it into their heads to cut the tradition, and gave their vote to a certain Captain Nolan, the *Home Rule* candidate. The irascible nobleman took revenge for what he chose to consider as a personal insult by raising the rent of all bad electors. He went so far in that line that in 1882 the *Land Commissioners* had to reduce them by half. That judgment could not, of course, have a retrospective effect and bring a restitution of the sums that had been paid in excess during the last ten years, and which varied from £50 to £100. It may be imagined how they must weigh still on the peasant's heart, and what a well-prepared ground the agrarian movement was to find at Woodford. The successive murders of the land agent

Blake and Bailiff Finlay were among the first and visible signs of that ferment of hatred.

Those crimes, which remained unpunished, and the responsibility of which is thrown at each other's heads by the two parties, came with the usual accompaniment of fires, mutilations, verbal and written threats. The reign of terror had begun in the district; no bailiff was any longer willing to serve a writ or assignation. There came a time when the landlords nearly gave up all hope of finding a land agent to take the place of the one who had been murdered; at last they discovered the man—a certain Joyce, of Galway—a man who united an indomitable spirit with the most consummate skill; deeply versed in the art of talking to the peasant, a fine shot, carrying his potations well; ready for anything. A professional exploit had made his name famous in the neighbourhood. Having to serve writs upon several farmers, and being unable to find bailiffs willing to carry them, he made a general convocation in his office of all the debtors, with the pretext of submitting to them some mode of accommodation. The proposition being unanimously rejected, Joyce gets up, goes to the door, and after having turned the key, leans with his back against it; then, producing out of his pocket as many writs as there were farmers in his room, distributes them among the visitors. The poor devils were caught; according to the terms of the law, nothing but submission was left to them. It will not be unnecessary to add here that Joyce, a born Catholic, had been recently converted to Protestantism, which is reputed an abomination in Ireland, and consequently went by the name of the *renegade*. Such was the man who came to settle at Loughrea under protection of a special guard of constables, and hostilities soon began.

The harvest of 1885 had been but indifferent, and besides, by reason of American competition, the price of the chief local products had fallen down considerably—from about 15 to 20 per cent.—which implies for the farmer an utter impossibility to pay his rent, unless the nett profit he draws from the soil be estimated above 15 or 20 per cent. of his general receipt. Even in Ireland reasonable landlords are to be found. Those who understood the situation felt for their tenants, and, without waiting to be asked, granted a reduction of rent. At Woodford, Lord Dunsandle and

Colonel Daly of their own impulse, and Sir H. Burke after some demur, gave up 15 per cent. of the unpaid rent.

As for Lord Clanricarde, he gave not the least sign of existence. When the November term came, his tenants demanded a reduction of 25 per cent., upon which Joyce declared that not a penny was to be given up. This seemed so hard that it was generally disbelieved; and an opinion spread itself that by applying personally to the landlord justice would be obtained. A collective address, signed by the 316 Woodford tenants, was accordingly drawn up and presented to him.

The Marquis of Clanricarde vouchsafed no manner of answer. Then, Father Egan put himself in motion. He first obtained from the Bishop of Clonfert that he would send a second petition to the master, representing to him the true state of affairs, the reduction consented to by the other landlords, &c. Lord Clanricarde did not even acknowledge reception of the prelate's letter. Let us state here, once for all, that he never swerved from the attitude he had adopted from the beginning, so aggressive in its very stolidity. Never once did he depart from that silence, except when he once wrote to the *Times* that, personally, he did not object to the proposed reduction, but was in the habit of leaving to his agent the care of that sort of thing.

Seeing that there was no satisfaction whatever to be expected from him, the Woodford tenants imitated their landlord, and henceforth gave no sign of life, or paid him a single farthing. In the month of April, 1886, Joyce resorted to the legal ways and set up prosecutions against thirty-eight of the principal farmers, whose debt was £20 and above, assuming by that move the attitude of a moderate man who has to deal with obvious unwillingness to pay.

And it was that which gave to the Woodford affair its peculiar character, which made it a *test case*, a decisive trial where the contending forces have measured their strength, where the inmost thought of the Irish peasant has shown itself in full light. If the chiefs of the League had singled it out from amidst a hundred (as, indeed, we may believe they did, whatever they might aver to the contrary), they could never have achieved a more complete demonstration of their power. Chance, however, had also its usual share in the turn which affairs took. Joyce, it appears, had began prosecutions against seventy-eight lesser tenants, and at the moment when success was on the point of crowning his efforts, the procedure was quashed for some legal flaw.

As for the bigger ones, judgment had been entered against them, and the execution followed. The first step was the selling out in public court of the tenant's interest in his holding. Ten of the men capitulated immediately, paying the rent in full with interest and law costs, that is to say, about 80 per cent. above the original debt. As for the twenty-eight others, fired by political passion, pride, and the ardent exhortations of Father Egan, they did not waver, and allowed the sale to proceed.

Agreeably to the usage established since the League has been supreme in Ireland, not one bidder came forward at the sale. The representative of the landlord therefore remained master of the situation, and got for a few shillings the interest of the twenty-eight farmers—interest which, in certain cases, was worth £200 and more.

It now remained to evict those tenants from their farms, and take possession in their place. Let us remark that, being certain of having allowed the landlord, through the sale, to help himself to a value of five or six times his due, those men were bound to consider such an eviction a gratuitous piece of cruelty. Well knowing before-hand that the eviction would by no means be an easy task, for all Ireland breathlessly followed the course of events, Joyce singled out amongst the twenty-eight defaulters, the four tenants for whom the eviction was sure to bear the hardest character, namely, Conroy, Fahey, Broderick, and Saunders. These were all people of comfortable means, who had for many years been established on their lands, who were profoundly attached to the house where their children or grand-children had been born, and which they had themselves built, enlarged and improved at great expense; rural *bourgeois* rather than peasants; men that in a French country town should have been mayors, *adjoints*, or municipal councillors.

For each of them eviction not only meant ruin, the voluntary and definitive loss of a small fortune laboriously acquired, and which could be estimated in each case at ten or twelve times the amount of the annual rent; it was, besides, the upsetting of all their dearest habits, the destruction of home, the end of domestic felicity. "Placed between this result and the choice of paying £30 or £40, which he has in his strong box, or which he will experience no difficulty in borrowing if he has them not—what country-bred man would hesitate?" thought Joyce. "Conroy, Fahey, Broderick, and Saunders shall pay! They shall pay, and after them the others must inevitably follow suit."

This was very sound reasoning. But Joyce calculated without the League and its agent, Father Egan. The four chosen victims did not pay. With a resolution that must really seem heroic to whoever knows the workings of a peasant's soul, Conroy, Fahey, Broderick, and Saunders unanimously declared that the agent might expel them by force—*if he could*—but yield they would not.

Ah! there was a fearful struggle. It was not without the most terrible inner combat that they kept their word. At home they had the money ready; nothing could be simpler than to go and pay it. Now and then temptation waxed almost too strong. James Broderick is an old man of seventy years. One day, called to Loughrea by the tempter, he went, in company with his friend Fahey.

"Now, look here, Mr. Broderick," Joyce said to him, "it goes to my heart to evict a good man like you from such a pretty house. . . . You have lived in it for these thirty years—it is the pearl of Woodford. . . . Let us make an arrangement about all this: you pay me down your rent with £2 for costs, and I give you any length of time for the rest. . . . His lordship will even give you back the tenant-right for the price he paid himself,—fifty shillings. . . . Now, what do you say?" . . . .

Old Broderick wavered; he was on the point of yielding.

"Indeed, Mr. Joyce, you cannot do more than that," ... he uttered in a trembling voice, involuntarily feeling for his pocket-book.

But Fahey was there. He took the old man's arm and drew him aside.

"It is not *time* that we want!" he said to him. "*What we want is to uphold the principle!*"

Truly a great word. As fine as any recorded on History's page, for those who know how to understand it rightly. If the peasants can remember a principle when their property is in question, verily one may say that the times are near being fulfilled!

All conciliatory means were now exhausted. It only remained to have recourse to force. Joyce knew better than anyone what resistance he was going to encounter. Personally he thought he was going to meet death. He went resolutely nevertheless, but not without surrounding himself with a regular army.

The bailiffs of the place refusing to act, some had to be sent for from Dublin. Those bailiffs, escorted by about a hundred emergency men, were supported besides by five hundred constables armed with rifles and revolvers. Woodford lies at a distance of about twenty miles from the nearest railway. The traps and horses necessary to carry all these people had to be sent down from Dublin, nobody consenting to give any manner of help. The same thing occurred for provisions and for the implements of the siege, pick-axes, levers, iron crowbars, which were indispensable to the assailants, and which were brought down with the army to Portumna. These preparations lasted three weeks. The mobilisation, decreed by Joyce at the end of July, could only be completed by the 17th of August.

On the next day, the 18th, this army moved forward and left Portumna in a column, marching on Woodford.

But on their side the Leaguers had not remained inactive.

All the night long squads of voluntary workmen had been hard at work. When the police caravan arrived in sight of the village, they found the road barred by trees and heaps of stones placed across the way. They were obliged to dismount and go round by the fields.

In the meantime, from the top of the neighbouring heights horns were signalling the appearance of the enemy; the chapel bells began to toll an alarm peal. From all the points of the compass an immense multitude of people hastened to come and take up their position on the hills of Woodford.

When the bailiffs made their appearance, headed by Joyce, armed to the teeth, by the under-sheriff whom the duty of his charge obliged to preside at the execution, and leading on five hundred policemen, an indescribable, formidable howl rose up to heaven; the Irish *wail* which partakes of the lion's roar and of the human sob, of the yell of the expiring beast and of the rushing sound of waters.

That lugubrious hooting was to last during two entire days, with full-stops, *da capo*, *decrescendo* and *rinforzando* of great effect.

The first house attacked by the assailants was that of Conroy. It is a solid, comfortable-looking dwelling, built on the bank of Lough Derg. To the under-sheriff's summons, the inhabitants, posted on the roof, answered only by derisive laughter. The door, which was of solid oak, was closed and barred inside. The order was given to break it open. A few minutes' work sufficed to do it.

When it fell crashing under the axes, it was perceived that a wall had been built behind it. . . . . A triumphant shout rose from the crowd.

"A breach must be made!" thundered Joyce. The stone wall was attacked. Immediately, from the roof, from the windows, poured a deluge of scalding hot lime-water, which fell on the assailants, blinded them, burnt them, and sent them back howling and dancing with pain. Again the crowd applauded, saluting with screams of laughter every ladleful of hot water that took effect. The custom of Galway authorizes, it appears, that singular way of defending one's house. *It is no breach of the peace.* One can scald the bailiffs without any qualms of conscience or fear of consequences.

Nothing loth, the Conroy family freely used the permission. The miracle was that they did not use more murderous weapons. But the League's agents were there holding back, according to their custom, the too fiery spirits, and keeping them within the bounds of legal hostilities. At their head the priest Egan was conspicuous, loudly advising the besieged, pointing out to them the uncovered assailants, telling them on what point to direct the effort of resistance. As for the police, mute and motionless, they beheld the drama without taking part in it. Four hours' work were needed to make the breach. At last the bailiffs were able to enter the house, expel the inhabitants, and take possession of it. They were obliged literally to carry away the youngest Miss Conroy, who desperately clung to the walls and furniture, and refused to come out of her own will.

Night came, and the bailiffs have no right to carry on their proceedings after sunset. They were therefore obliged to postpone their operations till the next day. What made matters worse was, that they must necessarily go back to Portumna, for they need expect to find no lodgings in Woodford. It is easy to foretell the complication of events that now followed.

The whole of next day was employed in the eviction of Fahey. That of Broderick lasted another day, and caused the arrest of twenty-seven persons, for in spite of the League's efforts heads were waxing hotter and hotter, and the combatants began to be rather too excited on both sides.

But where resistance took a truly epic character was in the house of Thomas Saunders. With twenty-three comrades he held in check all assaults *during four entire days.* Not content with scalding the bailiffs by means of pumps and cauldrons installed on purpose, he had, by a stroke of genius, the idea of throwing on them hives of bees, that came out enraged from their cells and cruelly stung everything before them. Who knows that there may not be in this a precious indication for future warfare! European strategists may before long add "the chaste dew-drinkers," as Victor Hugo called them, to the pigeons and the war-dogs. However that may be, Joyce's mercenaries, burnt, stung, and crest-fallen, were compelled, for three nights running, to retreat on Portumna.

The green flag meanwhile was proudly waving its folds on the summit of Saunders' house, which enraptured Ireland, intoxicated with joy at the news of this unprecedented siege, immediately baptized *Fort Saunders*. Agitation was fast spreading over the whole country. The military authorities judged it indispensable to send down 200 mounted men, and to have the place patrolled at night. In Portumna councils of war were held, and serious thoughts were entertained of having recourse to the antique battering-ram and "tortoise" in order to approach the place and succeed in taking it. Three days passed in new preparations and supplementary armaments.

At last, on the 27th of August, a new assault was attempted. It failed like all the others, but the law must, it was felt, at all costs, be enforced; the police interfered about some technical point, took the house at the bayonet's point and made all its inmates prisoners.

Thus ended, without effusion of blood, this memorable campaign; three weeks' preparation, eight days' fighting, a thousand men on foot, enormous expense had been required in order to succeed in evicting four tenants of the Marquis of Clanricarde, out of a number of 316, and that in the midst of scandalous scenes which gave the noisiest publicity to the agrarian cause. Everybody was of opinion that enough had been done, and evictions were stopped.

The affair at Woodford marks a date in the annals of the Irish revolution. One has seen in it peasants living in relatively good circumstances fight for principles and go to the furthest ends of legality,—without overstepping them. Moreover, these events have taken place in a county famed for its violence and represented in Parliament by Mr. Matthew Harris, which is saying enough; (his motto was, till lately, "When you see a landlord, shoot him down like a partridge"). Three or four years sooner such events could not have taken place without involving fifteen or twenty deaths of persons. Here not a single one occurred. One could not but acknowledge that the honour of this was due to the League, to its moderating and constitutional influence. In vain it protested that it had nothing to do with those conflicts; its agents and its general instructions played the first part in it. Therefore it reaped all the fruits of this, came out of the ordeal greater, surrounded with a poetical halo, sovereign. History often has such ironies. At the price of their domestic happiness, four obscure heroes had just won in face of public opinion the cause of the serfs of the glebe against the lords.

CHAPTER XV.

THE PLAN OF CAMPAIGN.

Sligo.

In all the cabins I enter, the first object that meets my eyes on the wall, besides a portrait of Parnell or Gladstone, is, enshrined between the bit of sacred palm and the photograph of the emigrant son, a sheet of printed paper, sometimes put under a glass, and headed by these words, "The Plan of Campaign." This is a summary of the instructions given by the League to its followers in November, 1886, and of the various means by which the position may be made untenable by the landlords.

That order of the day of the agrarian army was, however, absent from the house furniture of one of my friends, Mat Cloney; he was a fisherman on the Garvogue, near Lough Gill, and close to the ruins of the Abbey of Sligo; an old man of hale and pleasing countenance, whose weather-beaten face was shaded by a plenteous crop of gray hair, and lighted up by two wonderfully bright blue eyes: a true Celt in manner and appearance. When I entered his cabin for the first time he was engaged in preparing his dinner; this consisted of a dried herring and a cold potato; but tearing down from a hook near the fireplace a small piece of bacon, the old man hastily rubbed it over a frying-pan, which he set on the dying embers; in it he placed the herring. A great noise and spluttering followed, then Mat, mindful of future feasts, thriftily hung his piece of bacon back on its hook, and the herring being done, sat down to his meagre repast.

"You see, sir," he said contentedly, "it gives it a relish."

I must not omit to say that poor as his fare was, he nevertheless offered me a share of it. I explained I had already lunched, and while he was discussing his meal, we entered into conversation.

"You must be pretty well advanced in years," I said, "though one would not think it to see how you manage your boat."

"*Shure*, sir, I was *borren* in the *Ribillion!*"

Let me here observe that this is the common answer given by many Irish peasants as to their age. The "Ribillion" seems to have made an epoch in their history, and they consider that any person over middle age must have been born during that momentous period. The date appears to matter little to them. So, though I entertained private doubts of Cloney's being 89 years old, I let that pass, and we went on talking.

"Have you any children?"

"*Shure* I have! .... Me sons they are fishermen, and me daughters are all marr'd, near here. ..."

"And you live alone?"

"Yes, sir, that I do."

"It must be a lonely life for you. Were you never tempted to marry again after your wife's death? A fine man like you would have had no difficulty in finding a wife."

"Och, sir, after me ould woman died .... (with a burst of emotion) I always remained a *dacent widow-man* .... that I did! ...."

While we were talking I had been looking at the walls of the cabin, and I was surprised at finding none of the usual League's documents upon them. I turned to Mat and expressed my surprise. Instantly Mat let fall the knife with which he was conveying a piece of herring to his mouth, and burst into loud execrations.

"Och! the b——— villains!" he exclaimed; "the dirty never-do-well wh———! the de'il take them for his own! .... the whole lot is not worth a penny-worth o' salt; .... etc., etc."

I confess I rather wondered at this violence. But as everyone has a perfect right to his own opinion, I did not press the point.

"And you, sir, you be not English, are ye?" said Mat after a moment. He had suddenly grown calm again.

"No, I am French."

"Och! *Shure* the French are foine fellows. I had an uncle that fought the French for three days at Badajos, and he always said they were b——y devils, ... begging your pardon, sir, foine fellows they were. . . . . Me uncle always said so, ... under *Bonney* the French fought, ... b——d . . . . foine fellows, to be sure. . . . . Me uncle also said they had no landlords down there. Now, is that true, sir?" added Mat Cloney, looking at me with a queer expression of countenance.

No landlords? could that be true? He seemed to consider such a state of things suited to fairy-land.

I explained that this was pure truth. In few words I told him how, shortly before the *Ribillion* dear to his heart, the French peasants had risen as one man to get rid of their own landlords; how those landlords had for the most part emigrated and taken up arms against their country, which had caused the confiscation and sale of their lands. I added that those lands were now the property of the French labourers, who highly appreciate this state of affairs.

Mat Cloney listened to me, his eyes glistening with interest. Therefore, I was rather surprised when I stopped, and he abruptly asked me, as a conclusion:

"Do you know any of those Sligo gentlemen who come fishing about here, sir?"

"Indeed, I do not. I am a total stranger in these parts. It was the manager at my hotel who sent me to you."

"That's roight!" he exclaimed, as if relieved from some anxiety. "In that case, sir, I am going to show you something!..."

He went to a corner of the cabin, and after some rummaging in an old sailor's box, he produced from it a neatly folded paper which he placed into my hands. I opened it with some curiosity.

It was a supplementary sheet of the *United Ireland*, of Dublin, where stood *in extenso* the League's Plan of Campaign.

I looked at Mat Cloney. He was laughing silently. I at last understood the riddle. The sly fox was at heart with the League (he dubbed it *the Leg*, by the way, like many other Irishmen); but he judged it prudent in any case to dissemble such subversive feelings, when he had to do with an unknown person from the town ; and being a peasant he rather over-did it.

The ice was broken now. He let me study thoroughly the document he had lent me, and even enriched it with luminous commentaries, in the course of a pleasant day's fishing.

The "Plan of Campaign" seems to have had for its father Mr. John Dillon, one of the most universally, and the most deservedly, popular of the Irish members ; at all events, it was introduced to the public by that gentleman in October, 1886, at an autumn meeting. Those mass meetings, held every year after the harvest, have now become an institution, a kind of *Witena-gemot* of the Irish nation. People come to them from the farthest ends of the island, by rail, in jaunting-cars, on foot, on horseback, as the case may be ; in such numbers that there is no room or shanty large enough in the country to lodge the assemblage. So they are open-air meetings. The particular one alluded to was convened at Woodford, which has become, since the memorable battle on the Clanricarde estate, a kind of Holy Place and agrarian Kaaba. Soon after the autumn meeting, the scheme was approved by the authorities, at the head-quarters of the League (although they prudently refrained from committing themselves officially to it), and expounded in the special supplement to the *United Ireland,* of which I hold a copy. It was to the following effect :—

Present rents, speaking roundly, are impossible. That the landlords will press for them is certain. A fight for the coming winter is therefore inevitable, and it behoves the Irish tenantry to fight with a skill begotten by experience. The first question they have to consider is how to meet the November demand. Should combinations be formed on the lines of branches of the National League, or merely by estates? We say *by estates* decidedly. Let branches of the National League, if they will, take the initiative in getting the tenantry on each estate to meet one another. But it should be distinctly understood that the action or resolution of one estate was not to bind any other, and the tenantry on every estate should be free to decide upon their own course.

When they are assembled together, let them appoint an intelligent and sturdy member of their body as chairman, and, after consulting, decide by resolution on the amount of abatement they will demand. A committee consisting, say, of six and the chairman, should then be elected, to be called a Managing Committee, and to take charge of the half-year's rent of the tenant, should the landlord refuse it.

Everyone should pledge himself (1) to abide by the decision of the majority; (2) to hold no communication with the landlord or any of his agents, except in presence of the body of the tenantry; (3) to accept no settlement for himself which is not given to every tenant on the estate.

On the rent-day, the tenantry should proceed to the rent-office in a body. If the agent refuses to see them in a body, they should on no account confer with him individually, but depute the chairman to act as their spokesman and acquaint them of the reduction which they require. No offer to accept the rent "on account" should be agreed to. Should the agent refuse, then EVERY TENANT MUST HAND TO THE MANAGING COMMITTEE THE HALF-YEAR'S RENT WHICH HE TENDERED TO THE AGENT.

To prevent any attempt at a garnishee, this money should be deposited by the Managing Committee with some one reliable person, *whose name would not be known to any but the members of the committee.*

This may be called the estate fund, and it should be absolutely at the disposal of the Managing Committee for the purposes of the fight. Broken tenants who are unable to contribute the reduced half-year's rent should at least contribute the percentage demanded from the landlord, that is the difference between the rent demanded and that which the tenantry offer to pay. A broken tenant is not likely to be among the first proceeded against, and no risk is incurred by the general body in taking him on these terms.

Thus, practically a half-year's rent of the estate is put together to fight the landlord with. This is a fund which, if properly utilised, will reduce to reason any landlord in Ireland.

How should the fund be employed? The answer to this question must to some extent depend upon the course the landlord will pursue; but in general we should say it must be devoted to the support of the tenants who are dispossessed either by sale or ejectment.

It should be distributed by the committee to each evicted tenant in the proportion of his contribution to the fund. A half-year's rent is supposed to maintain a tenant for a half year, and based upon this calculation, a tenant who funded say £50 would be entitled when evicted to receive £2 per week.

But not one penny should go in law costs. This should be made an absolute rule. For to pay law costs, such as attorney's letters, writs and judgments incurred by the landlord, is to arm your enemy for the quarrel and furnish him with provisions to boot. In a determined fight there are no "law costs" on the side of the tenantry, and they should remain out for ever rather than pay those which the landlord incurs in fleecing them.

Ejectment is the most common of the landlord's remedies. Every legal and constitutional obstacle which could oppose or delay eviction should be had recourse to, for every hour by which the sheriff is delayed in one eviction gives another brother tenant so much more grace. There are only 310 days in the sheriff's year, and he must do all the evictions in a whole county within the time.

If, after eviction, a tenant is re-admitted as caretaker he should go in, but *never* upon the understanding that he would care any other farm but his own. Should the tenant not be re-admitted, shelter must be procured for him immediately by the Managing Committee, and then, if necessary, a day appointed when all would assemble to build him a hut on some spot convenient to the farm where the landlord could not disturb him. Wooden huts, such as those supplied by the League, waste too much of the funds and become valueless when the tenant is re-admitted.

Sale is the resort of the landlord when he proceeds by writ or process as an ordinary creditor. From eight to twelve days are allowed after service of the writ before judgment can be marked. The sheriff may seize cattle if he finds them on the farm, or he may seize and sell the tenant's interest in the farm. A tenant who has his mind made up for the fight will have his cattle turned into money before the judgment comes on. Every tenant who neglects to dispose of them is preparing himself to accept the landlord's terms, for he will not wish to see the emergency men profit by taking his cattle at some nominal price, and if he buys he is in reality handing the landlord the amount of his demand. Sale of a farm is not of so much consequence. Every farm sold in this manner during the agitation either has come or is bound to come back to its owner even on better terms than he first held it. But if a man has a very valuable interest in his farm, he can place it beyond the sheriff's power by mortgaging it to some one to whom he owes money. Mortgage effected thus for a *bonâ fide* debt or consideration bars the sheriff's power of conveyance at a sale. If the landlord or emergency men be represented, the cattle should not be allowed to go at a nominal sum. They should be run up to their price, and, if possible, left in the hands of emergency men at full price. It should be borne in mind that if the full price be not realised the sheriff could seize again for the balance.

In bidding for a farm it should also be run to amount of debt, but by a man of straw, or some one who, if it were knocked down, would ask the sheriff for time to pay. By making the landlord's bidder run it up to the amount of debt and costs, and leaving it on his hands, the sheriff cannot follow the tenant further. No auction fees should be allowed. A farm held on a lease for a life or lives, any one of which is extant, cannot be sold by the sheriff. After sale a tenant is still in possession of holding until a fresh writ is served and a judgment for title marked against him. All this involves the landlord in fresh costs. The eviction may then follow, and the observations above recorded in case of ejectment or eviction apply here.

Distress, another of the landlord's remedies, cannot be resorted to for more than one year's rent. Few landlords can have recourse to this without exposing themselves to actions. The chief points to attend to are :—That distress must be made by landlord or known agent, or bailiff authorized by warrant signed by the landlord or known agent ; that particulars of distress be served ; seizure on Sunday is unlawful ; seizure before sunrise or after sunset is unlawful; or for any rent due more than one year. Distress is illegal if growing crops be seized, or the implements of a man's trade ; and if other property be on farm to ensure landlord's demand, it is illegal to seize beasts of the plough, sheep, or implements of husbandry necessary for the cultivation of the land. These points should be carefully watched when landlord has recourse to distress.

Bankruptcy proceedings are too costly a machinery for general use, and no landlord is likely to have recourse to them.

It is unnecessary to add that landlords, and their partisans on the magisterial bench and among the Crown officials, will do all in their power to twist the operation of the law so as to harass the tenants.

A tenant taking possession of his house to shelter his family from the severity of the winter is not likely to escape. A summons for trespass must be preceded by a warning to the tenant if he be found in possession. We have known a case where the father complied with this warning, and on the bailiff's next visit the mother only was found, and she complied. Next time the eldest daughter only was in possession, and so on through the length of a long family, such as an evicted tenant nearly always has. A goodly time had been saved before the father's turn came again. He was fined and went to gaol. The prison then lost its terror for him. When he came out he stuck boldly to his home, and he soon won the victory which rewards determination.

The fullest publicity should be given to evictions, and every effort made to enlist public sympathy. That the farms thus unjustly evicted will be left severally alone, and every one who aids the eviction shunned, is scarcely necessary to say. But the man who tries boycotting for a personal purpose is a worse enemy than the evicting landlord, and should be expelled from any branch of the League or combination of tenants. No landlord should get one penny rent on any part of his estates, wherever situated, so long as he has one tenant unjustly evicted. This policy strikes not only at the landlord but the whole ungodly crew of agents, attorneys, and bum-bailiffs. Tenants should be the first to show their sympathy with one another, and prompt publicity should be given to every eviction, that the tenants of the evictor wherever he holds property may show their sympathy.

Such a policy indicates a fight which has no half-heartedness about it, and it is the only fight which will win.

Well may the author of the "Plan of Campaign" wind up his catechism by the appropriate remark that "such a policy indicates a fight which has no half-heartedness about it." Never before was such a tremendous weapon of social war put in motion. Never before, in the whole course of history, was such a forcible ultimatum drafted for the consideration of the adverse party.

Leaving details aside, and the minute instructions on the true mode of skirmishing with the myrmidons of the law, the idea of using the very rent claimed by the landlord as a provision for feeding the struggle against him is in itself perfection—a real masterpiece of strategy. An artist can only feel the warmest admiration for such a combination of everything that is most pleasant to the heart of the agrarian warrior and most deadly to the landlord's cause. As an orator of the League (Mr. W. O'Brien) has put it: "We have discovered a weapon against landlordism, the mere threat and terror of which have already brought down rack-renters to their knees. We have discovered a weapon which feudal landlordism can no more resist than a suit of armour of the middle ages can resist modern artillery." And the country where such an admirable paper has been penned by its political leaders is supposed by its foes to be unable to rule its own affairs! This is unfairness with a vengeance. Let those meet its provisions, since they are so very clever.

The wonder, however, is not that such a policy should have been dreamed of. Similar plans of warfare have more than once been drawn out in the council chamber of parties. The wonder is that this one should have been deemed practicable by the farmers of Ireland; that it should have been unanimously accepted by them; and, what is more, put at once into effect. Another wonder is that it should have been found *lawful*, on the best legal authority, and that it should have remained unopposed by the "Four Courts" and "the Castle." The greatest wonder of all is that it should have enlisted the warm and public support not only of the lower ranks of the clergy all over the island, but of the Episcopate itself; not only of the Episcopate but of the Pope, since neither his special envoy in Ireland nor his Holiness personally in any encyclical letter, have spoken one word in condemnation of the "Plan of Campaign."

It has been in operation now for over one year; it has spread as far as the leaders of the League have deemed it expedient, for thus far they seem to have used it only moderately. "We did not desire," they say, "and we do not desire now that the 'Plan of Campaign' should be adopted anywhere, except where the tenants have a just and moderate and unimpeachable case." But, none the less, it hangs as a formidable threat over the heads of the doomed landlords. At a moment's notice it may be extended to the whole island, as it has been already to some hundred estates in twenty-two counties.

An idea of the state of affairs may be gathered from the account given by the *Freeman's Journal* (December 3, 1886) of the scene witnessed on Lord de Freyne's property in county Sligo. His tenants asked for an abatement of 20 per cent., and, being refused, they decided to adopt the "Plan of Campaign."

The Plan of Campaign.

There is nothing in the nature of a town or even a village at Kilfree Junction, there being only two or three one-story thatched cottages within sight of it. In one of these, the nearest to the station, the rents were received by Mr. William Redmond, M.P.; the Rev. Canon O'Donoghue, D.D.; Rev. Father Henry, C.C.; and the Rev. Father Filan, C.C. The operations of receiving the rents, entering amounts, and giving receipts to the tenants occupied the greater part of the day, commencing in early morning and continuing far in the afternoon. Although the situation was rather a depressing one for the poor people exposed to all the severity of the elements, they seemed to be one and all animated by the greatest enthusiasm. The interior of the cottage in which the rents were being collected presented a spectacle really unique in its way. The first room, a sort of combination of kitchen, sitting-room, and shop, was crowded almost to suffocation by men and a few women, who were sheltering from the snow which fell in great white flakes without. There was no grate, but a few turf sods burned on the hearth, while above them hung a kettle, suspended from an iron hook fixed from the quaint old chimney. In the centre of the bedroom leading off the apartment was a small table, at which Mr. Redmond, M.P., the clergymen whose names are given above, and one of the leading members of the local branch of the National League were seated receiving the tenants' rents. The room was densely crowded, but the utmost order and decorum prevailed, and the whole proceedings were conducted in the most punctilious and business-like manner.

The tenant handed the money to one of the gentlemen at the table, his name was duly entered with the amount paid by him into a book, and he was handed back a printed receipt for the amount which he had lodged.

As the day wore on, the pile of bank notes upon the table mounted higher and higher, and the rows of glistening sovereigns grew longer and longer, until they stretched across the table like streams of yellow ore. It was difficult to realise how those bleak western plains had ever produced so much money, and the conviction seemed to force itself upon the mind that a considerable part of it had either been earned by work across the Channel, or in remittances from friends and relations on the other side of the broad Atlantic.

"Father," exclaimed one of the younger men, pushing excitedly his aged parent into the room where the rents were being paid over, "come along ; you have lived to strike a blow for freedom and Ireland." The words were uttered with earnestness and enthusiasm. There are upwards of 300 tenants upon this estate alone who have adopted the "Plan," and a further sitting will be necessary in order to receive the remaining lodgments.

A couple of policemen, who looked chilled and spiritless, walked about the platform, but made no attempt to interfere with the proceedings.

It would be useless to add the least comment to such a picture. When similar scenes are witnessed everywhere over a country, and accepted by every one as the natural consummation of events, and the law is impotent to prevent them, the Revolution is not impending—it is practically accomplished in the mind of all classes.

CHAPTER XVI.

SCOTTISH IRELAND.

ENNISKILLEN.

IF you did not know beforehand that you are entering a new Ireland through Enniskillen, an Ireland, Scotch, Protestant, manufacturing, a glance through the carriage-window would suffice to reveal the fact. Over the hill, on the right, a fine country-house waves to the wind, as a defiance to the League, his orange-coloured flag, the colours of the "*Unionists.*" The landlords of Leinster, Munster, and Connaught, who are Orangemen, as well as others, dare not proclaim their opinions so boldly, hoist them at the top of the main mast, so to say; for it might simply cost them their lives. You must come to "loyal Ulster" to see such acts of daring, for the simple reason that they are without danger here.

Another symptom, more eloquent still than the colour of the flag, is the aspect of the landscape; no more uncultivated fields, no more endless bogs and fens. Instead of those long, red, or black streaks of peat, alternating with consumptive oat and potato-fields, green, fat meadows, mown by steam, studded with cows, in the most prosperous condition, spread themselves before your eyes. Some trees are to be seen now. The hedges are in good repair, the horses well harnessed to solid carts; the hay-stacks have a symmetrical outline, and vast fields of flax nod under the breeze; the farm-houses are well built, flanked by neat kitchen-gardens; in short, all gives the general impression of a properly cultivated land. Nothing like the agricultural opulence of Kent or Warwickshire though, but the normal state of a tolerably good land, where human industry is not fighting against an accumulation of almost insuperable obstacles.

Is it that the law is different in Ulster? Not so, but the custom is. From immemorial times the tenant-right has been admitted here; and in consequence the farmer has never hesitated to introduce the necessary improvements, and to invest his hoard in the land, sure as he is to profit by it.

That tenant is three times out of five of Scotch origin; three times out of five he belongs to the Protestant persuasion (Episcopal, Presbyterian, Methodist); there is not between him and his landlord the antagonism of race and worship which is to be found in other provinces. The landlord himself fulfils his duty better, and does not affect to spend abroad the money he draws from his estate ; often that landlord is some guild or municipal corporation of London or elsewhere, which perhaps does not make the best use possible of its income, but is nevertheless obliged to justify more or less its privilege by some philanthropic foundation, trials of culture on the large scale, innovation, and examples.

Lastly, Ulster is a neighbour to Scotland, and belongs to the same geological, ethnological, commercial, and religious system. Capital is less timorous here. It ventures to come, to stay, to circulate. By the side of agriculture there are important factories, which help to sustain and feed it. Instead of keeping invariably to oats, turnips, and the time-honoured potato, the farmers grow flax on a large scale for the 400,000 spindles which are spinning at Belfast, Dundalk, and Drogheda.

A certain tendency to aggregate small holdings, and to constitute in that way great and middling farms, has been developing lately in Ulster. The peasants are better lodged and fed than elsewhere in Ireland They find day-work more easily because agriculture is conducted there on more scientific principles, and they are not condemned to remain idle four days out of seven. In short, the economic condition of Scotch Ireland, without being such as to be offered as a pattern to the civilised world, is about as good as possible under the feudal *régime* and landlordism.

LONDONDERRY.

The signs of that relative prosperity are obvious. Thus in the neighbourhood of Derry (we say Londonderry, but the natives all say Derry), you observe with pleasure a line of tramcars moved by steam machinery, which puts remote places in communication with the railway. The carriages are of superior make, divided into three classes, towed by an engine heated with petroleum. Coming, as you do, out of Mayo and Galway, that steam tramway puffs in your face a breath of civilisation. You seem to enter a different world.

Derry, with its active traffic, its elegant iron bridge over the Foyle, the fine, new buildings which attest its wealth, justifies that impression. It is the capital of the famous "Ulster plantation" of James I., entrusted by him to the "Honourable Irish Company," which included twelve guilds of the city of London. For a century or two those grants of land did not answer as had been expected. But they have ended, in the course of time, by being prosperous. The municipal estates of Coleraine and Derry are accounted now the most flourishing in the island.

Yet it does not follow that the tenant's situation is very brilliant, even in Ulster. One of the counties of the province, Donegal, is the poorest in all Ireland, and two or three others are not much better. Even in the richest parts the tenant bears chafingly the yoke of landlordism. The Antrim Tenant Association went so far this year as to ask for a 50 per cent. reduction on rent, owing to the low price of produce and the sheer impossibility of going on paying at the previous rate. It must be noted that tenant-right being rigorously observed in Ulster, the farmer always pays when he is able; for any remissness in paying would diminish by as much the value of his share in the proprietorship, which is estimated on an average at 8 or 10 times the annual farm rent.

The newspapers of the county, even when unfavourable to agrarian revendications, unanimously acknowledge that by reason of the constant going down of prices, resulting from American competition, the present condition of the agriculturist is about as bad as it was in the worst famine times. All the farmers without exception, be they of Scotch or

Irish race, aver that they actually pay from their own pockets every penny they give the landlords; that is to say, they borrow it in the shape of a loan on the value of their tenant-right.

Such a state of things cannot continue. It explains how it is that Presbyterian peasants, the most ardent enemies of Papistry—in theory—none the less give the majority, even in Ulster itself, to the representatives of Home Rule and the liquidation of landed property.

Portrush and the Giant's Causeway.

Portrush is a delicious sea-side place, at the mouth of Lough Foyle, on the most wonderful coast in Europe; it is seated on the edge of the Antrim table-land, which is of volcanic origin: probably a dependency of Scotland geologically, rather than belonging properly to Ireland, to which it came and welded itself, at some unknown epoch. The traveller has there the agreeable surprise of a delightful hotel —one should say a perfect one—a regular miracle of comfort; and the still greater surprise of seeing there the only electric railway actually working on this planet. That bijou-line is used to take the visitors to the wonder of Ireland, the Giant's Causeway. It ascends on the sea-side an acclivity of about three to four hundred yards, and runs over a length of five miles up to Bushmills, where the generators of electricity are set to work by hydraulic power. Nothing is so fresh or unexpected as that drive in open carriages. The train ascends lustily along the electric guiding-rail in the midst of a well-nourished fire of sparkles called to life by its iron hoofs. As it rises higher the prospect gets wider and wider, and you get a view of the Scotch mountains only fifteen miles distant, while the most extraordinary basaltic formations are following one another under your eye along the coast.

The Antrim table-land, so geologists tell us, was formed by a layer of lava three or four hundred yards high, spread over the chalky bottom of the sea. Of the volcanoes which vomited that lava no vestige is to be seen to-day. The glaciers, tumbling down from the neighbouring heights, have cleared them away. In times remote, that table-land extended across to Scotland, to which it united Ireland as by a sort of prodigious bridge of lava. But the unremitting, incessant, work of the waters has eaten away by degrees the cretaceous masses which supported it.

The arches of the bridge were then dislocated and precipitated into the ocean. Only some traces of it on both sides are left standing now: the Giant's Causeway in Ireland, the point of Cantire in Scotland, and between the two, the little Island of Rathlin.

Along the coast of Antrim the waves continuing their destructive work, go on gnawing the foundations of the cliffs, which they dig and carve like lacework. Numberless grottoes, rocky needles shaped into the likeness of steeples, deep chasms at the bottom of which the foaming waters are for ever contending, are the result of that perennial work.

Occasionally, as at Dunluce, to the fantastic work of nature, some ruin that was once an illustrious stronghold, whose walls, literally hanging over the abyss, seem to be attached to the firm ground only by a curved arch of half-a-yard's breadth, adds an element of tragic poetry. Under the rock which bear those dilapidated walls, the sea has dug for itself caves which are resounding night and day with the deafening noise of the beating waves. It is grand and terrible in summer; one can imagine what it must be when the tempest of a winter night unloosens its fury within those caverns.

Naturally they are, more than any other place in the world, rich in legendary lore. The M'Quillans, to whom belonged Dunluce Castle, boast an antiquity which outshines greatly that of the descendants of the Crusaders. These are not people to be content, like Montesquieu, with two or three hundred years of acknowledged nobility. They came from Babylon, it appears, at an epoch exceptionally prehistoric, and can trace their origin back to 4,000 years ago. The only branch in existence now dwells in Scotland, and bear the title of lords of Antrim and Dunluce.

At Bushmills the electric train stops. There you alight and take your seat in the car which brings you to the Causeway Hotel. Here, as the air is decidedly bracing, and the majority of the tourists English, luncheon is ready, as you may imagine. The classic salmon despatched in company with a glass of ale or porter, the only thing to do is to look to business and visit the marvels of the place. A wall, which the provident administration of the hotel have raised for purposes of safety, hides them as yet from your sight. When you have passed that obstacle you find yourself within a sort of circus, delineated by the cliffs, and at the extremity of which descends a path that looks anything but safe.

Total absence of causeway. Where must we look for it? This a swarm of guides, cicerones, boatmen, beggars of all descriptions, offer to show you. They all speak at the same time, fight, wrangle, make you deaf with their jabbering. Wise is he who sends them to the devil, and follows peacefully the pathway which goes to the extremity of the circuit, turns alone round the foot of the cliff on the right, and penetrates, unaccompanied, into the neighbouring bay. He will have the joy of a powerful, wholly personal sensation, unalloyed by any impure element. But alas! how is one to guess that? You think you are doing the right thing in giving the lead to a professional guide. You choose among the howling crew the less ruffianly face, and you deliver yourself into the hands of a cicerone. Fatal error! Henceforward you cease to belong to yourself. You are no longer a being endowed with reason and volition, with the free exercise of your rights; you are an article of luggage in the hands of a porter, a disarmed traveller in the power of a Calabrian desperado.

Instead of taking you to the bay on the right, the arbiter of your destiny begins by laying down as a dogma that the only means of seeing the causeway properly is to approach it by sea. On the same occasion you shall visit the marine caves. Allured by that programme, you follow the man, and you embark with him in a boat rowed by two oarsmen, who greet your advent rapturously.

Five minutes later you find yourself in total darkness under the oozing vault of a cavern, where the fluctuations of the mountainous waves now let the boat sink suddenly five or six yards down, now heave it up against the roof, and threaten to shiver your skull to pieces. In the midst of that frantic jogging and tossing the guide lights up a Bengal flame, in order to display to better advantage the variegated tints of the damp walls, or, it may be, to create the said tints, if they do not exist. Then he lets off a pistol in your ear to awake the echoes of the cavern, which answer to the call with deafening unanimity.

This is the "psychological moment." The rowers, laying down their oars, take off their caps and hold them to you, explaining at the same time that gunpowder is expensive. You hasten to accede to the request, and soon after you find yourself, not without pleasure, in the daylight again.

Not for long, however; for you are expected to do another cavern. You submit meekly to the programme. Again that homicidal tossing; another

Bengal flame; a second pistol shot. This time the boatmen offer you a box of geological specimens. As it is, you happen to abhor geology; but how is one to resist people who have him in their power in a marine cave?

Liberation comes in time. You breathe again. The miscreants have the face to mention a third cavern! But this time you rebel. "No more caverns! The causeway instantly!"

You double a little promontory, and after two or three oar-strokes you land on what seems to you at first a quay with a pavement made with hexagon slabs.

"Here you are, sir! This is the Giant's Causeway." Let us confess it candidly: the first impression is disappointment. Is it then that famous Causeway, that unrivalled wonder? You are ready to believe in a mystification. But this is only a passing impression for which the guides, not the Causeway, are responsible.

The truth is, you must not approach it by sea if you wish to see it well. It is by land only that it can be understood, like a symphony which would lose half its charm if executed in the open air. The treason of the guides is so cruel that it really cries for vengeance and must be denounced.

At last you have managed to get rid of them, and leaving the Causeway, you have climbed up the steep neighbouring cliffs. And now looking round, you are struck with stupefaction and rapture at the spectacle which offers itself to your eyes. That sort of quay or footpath you deemed at first mean or insignificant is in reality, when viewed properly, the most stupendous whim of nature. Imagine a formidable array of forty thousand columns of prismatic shape (some one gifted with patience has numbered them), rising tall and majestic, and pressed against each other so as to form a continuous, almost level pavement, which emerges from the sea like a quay of marble. The symmetry of that pavement is so remarkable, all those shafts of columns are so well clamped together, that it seems almost impossible to admit that this is not human work. You fancy you are walking on the hexagonal slabs of some Babylonian palace, whose walls the storm has destroyed. These paving-stones are neat and even, about one foot wide, and perfectly regular. Towards the middle of the quay they rise in a sort of swelling, which permits one to study their anatomy and to perceive that they are really formed by the section of as many upright parallel prismatic columns.

There are three Causeways,—the Great, the Little, and the Middle Causeway. They occupy the centre of a semi-circular bay, formed by lofty cliffs, which let you see under a thin covering of clay and grass other rows of basaltic columns that show their profile, and have been called "the Organ." On the right the bay is limited by a jutting rock, above which tower two or three needles—"the Chimney-pots." A local tradition relates that the Invincible Armada, driven against the cliffs by a strong gale, mistook the needles for the towers of Dunluce, and stormed them uselessly a whole day long.

Beyond those basaltic piers a spring of sweet water forms the "Giant's Well;" further on a rock, roughly shaped as a church desk, is called "the Pulpit." All those sports of nature compose a whole truly unique and wonderful. Neither the Alps, nor the chain of the Andes, nor Mount Vesuvius, nor Etna, can give you such an impression of grandeur—are able to that degree to put you as it were into communion with the mysteries of labouring Nature.

What strikes you further about those basaltic formations is that they are both colossal, like all works directly resulting from the great cosmic forces, and at the same time almost Greek by the quality and symmetry of their arrangements. For once the volcanos seem to have had the whim to work according to the canons of art. It is both human and super-human—verily a Giant's Causeway!

The Giant Fin M'Coul, so the legend says, was the guardian genius of Ireland. He had for a rival a certain Scotch Giant of mighty conceit and insolence, whose boast it was that none could beat him. The sea alone, if that Scotch braggart was to be believed, prevented his coming to let M'Coul feel the might of his arm, as he was afraid of getting a cold if he attempted to swim across the Straits. So he remained at home. M'Coul was riled at last by that swaggering. "Since thou art afraid to get wet," he cried to his rival, "I am going to throw a causeway between Scotland and Ireland, and we shall see then whether thou darest use it!" The building of the bridge took only a few thousand years, and then the Scot, having no pretence left, accepted the challenge, was beaten flat, and obliged to eat humble pie. After which, with true Irish generosity, the good-natured giant gave him his daughter in marriage, and allowed him to come and settle near him, which the Scot accepted, nothing loth, Erin being an infinitely sweeter and generally superior country to his own. But perhaps, after all, M'Coul found no cause to rejoice over the match he had arranged for his daughter, as he subsequently allowed the sea to destroy his work so as to prevent any more Scots from settling in his dominions. Only some of its piles remain standing, one of which is the Isle of Rathlin, half-way across the Straits.

The legend, as you see, is not so foolish. It answers at all points to geological data, and even to historic truth, viz., the invasion of Ulster by the Scots. But, let its origin be what it may, the fact remains that the Giant's Causeway, with its neighbour, Portnoffen Bay, the most perfect amphitheatre in the world, with the marvellous colonnade of the Pleaskin, Dunluce Castle, Dunseverick, and the bridge of rope of Carrick-a-Rede, thrown over a chasm that measures a hundred feet above the waters,—constitute one of the grandest, most moving spectacles that the traveller may see. You can go round the world without having such extraordinary sights. Add to it that few of the gems of nature are of so easy an access. From Paris you can be on the coast of Antrim in twenty hours, by London, Liverpool, and Belfast. Portrush, with its admirable sea-shore, its electric railway, and stupendous cliffs, is the ideal frame for a honeymoon excursion. I had resolved to recommend it to tourists, and to point out the guides of the Causeway to public execration. Now I have done my duty.

BELFAST.

The capital of Ulster is naturally the most flourishing town of Ireland. Whereas the others decrease in population and wealth, Belfast is rapidly thriving. From 20,000 inhabitants, which it numbered at the beginning of the century, it has risen in eighty years to 210,000. Another ten years and it will outdo Dublin itself. It is a manufacturing city as well as a big trading port. By an exception, unique in the island, it occupies a great number of workers, male and female—60,000, at the lowest computation—for the most part, in the weaving trade and naval construction. A single linen factory, that of Messrs. Mulholland, gives work to 29,000 pairs of hands. It is those weaving looms which utilize the product of the 110,000 acres of flax fields in Ulster. Out of nineteen ships of over 300 tons annually built in the docks of the island eighteen come out of the Belfast wharves. It is, in short, the maritime gate of Irish import and export—the insular suburb of Liverpool and Glasgow.

As a consequence, signs of prosperity are showing themselves everywhere. The public walks are vast and carefully kept, the houses well built, the shops substantial and elegant, the educational establishments important and richly endowed. The town has a thoroughly Anglo-Saxon aspect. London fashions are scrupulously followed there. If you enter the Botanical Garden, maintained by voluntary contributions, you find there the lawn-tennis, the dresses, the ways of the metropolis. If you follow the road up to Cave Hill, one of the heights on the western side of Belfast, you embrace a vast landscape, where the flying steamers on the Lagan, the smoking factory-chimneys, the innumerable and opulent villas round its shores, all speak of wealth and prosperity.

The population is about equally divided between Protestants and Catholics. The consequence is that party hatred and the struggle for local influence are far more ardent and long-lived here than in places where one of the two elements has an overwhelming majority. Electoral scuffles easily turn to bloody battles; political anniversaries—that of the Battle of the Boyne, above all—are a pretext for manifestations which often degenerate into regular battles.

Belfast is the bulwark of Orangeism; and Orangeism may be described as Protestant and loyalist fanaticism, as opposed to Catholic and national fanaticism. Shankhill Road, which is frequently used as a battle-field by the antagonistic parties, is a long suburb which divides as a frontier line the Orangeist from the Irish quarters.

Hardly one pay-day passes without the public-houses of that suburb being the theatre of some pugilistic feat accomplished by some voluntary representatives of the opposite camps. If the police happen to rush into the fray, reinforcements are called from either side; stones, cudgels, revolvers come to the rescue, and, on the morrow, the jails are filled with prisoners, and the hospitals with the dead and the wounded.

Sad to relate, it is the clergy on both sides who incite them to those fratricidal struggles. There are certain Protestant preachers who are in no way behindhand in bitterness and virulent abuse with the most fanatic priest of Roscommon or Mayo. I have heard personally in Falls Road a Methodist preaching in the open air incite his audience to the extermination of Papists in strains which the creatures of Cromwell would not have disowned.

In order that nothing should be missing to the parallel, Ulster has its Orangeist League, not unlike the National League of Ireland (save for the respect of legality and the general moderation of proceedings). That League is formed into battalions and companies which are privately drilled, they say, and lose no occasion to make a pageant in the streets with accompaniment of trumpets and drums, and whose ways remind one of the Salvation Army.

On the whole, Ulster is the only province of Ireland where the Unionist forces are about equally matched with the party of Home Rule; that is to say, the former command a majority in Antrim, part of Down, part of Armagh, part of Derry and Donegal, whilst the Home Rulers have the stronger array of voters in the remaining parts of the province. Except in the above-delineated band of north-eastern territory, the result of the elections is always taken for granted beforehand all over the island, and is for—Home Rule. But this is not saying that the contest is at all passionate even in Belfast. I happened to be there on the occasion of the General Election of 1886, and was most struck by the comparative calm of the population pending the momentous ballot. I could not help expressing my surprise, over the mahogany, to my host, a wealthy mill-owner, a zealous Presbyterian, and an active Orangeist into the bargain, to whom an English friend had given me a letter of introduction.

"You wonder at our calm?" he said. "The explanation is very simple. In Ireland the respective position of parties can hardly be much altered by the incidents of the struggle. Whether the Home Rulers take one seat from us or we gain one on them, we shall neither of us be much benefited by it. It is in Great Britain that the true battle is taking place. Let us suppose that Mr. Gladstone, instead of finding himself in a minority in the next Parliament, returns to the House with a majority. This majority can in no case be very strong, and we may still doubt that it will consent to follow him to the end in the path he has chosen. But let us go farther, and suppose Home Rule to have been voted by this majority,—let us suppose it to have been voted by the Upper House,—a still more unlikely contingency. Well, our decision is taken irrevocably. We are perfectly resolved not to bow to such a vote, and not to submit to Home Rule."

"What! shall you rebel against the constitution?"

"Against the constitution, no. But if needs must be against Mr. Gladstone and his party. We shall appeal from the ignorant electors to the better informed ones. We shall protest against a decision that would in a way deprive us of our rights as British subjects. And in the meanwhile we shall refuse to acknowledge a Dublin Parliament. We shall refuse to pay the taxes that it may fix upon, or to obey the laws it may vote. We shall repeat loudly that we are Englishmen, and will not be anything else; that we depend on the British Parliament and recognize no other authority; and we shall see then if our appeal raise no echo in the United Kingdom!"

"But still, the right of making laws generally entails the power of enforcing them. What shall you do on the day when the Dublin Parliament, having voted the taxes for you as for the rest of Ireland, shall send tax-gatherers to collect them?"

"*We shall receive them with rifle-shots.*"

"What! are you going to tell me that you, sir, 'worth' half a million sterling, if the public voice speaks the truth, that this fat gentleman there, the father of those two pretty daughters, that this respectable doctor in gold spectacles, and all your other guests to-night, all peace-loving, middle-aged gentlemen, comfortable and with good rent-rolls, seriously entertain the idea of buckling on your shooting-gaiters and going to battle in the street?"

"We shall go, if we are obliged, rather than submit to the Dublin people! . . . After all, have we not a right to remain English, if it suits us? ... The very principle of Home Rule, if it is adopted, implies that we shall govern ourselves as it seems good to us. Well, here in Ulster, we are nearly two million loyalist Protestants, who cherish the pretension of not being given over to the three million Papists entrusted with the making of the Dublin Parliament,—who shall dare to deny this right to us?"

"Mr. Parnell and his friends will certainly deny it as soon as their programme is embodied into law. They will say to you, 'Henceforth Ireland shall govern herself. Let those who do not like it go away.'"

"But it is precisely what we shall never do! ... Our title to the Irish soil is as good as the Parnellites' ... Let them try to dislodge us, and they shall have a warm welcome, I promise you."

In the course of conversation my worthy interlocutor had let the number of 100,000 Orangemen, armed to the teeth and ready to defend Ulster against the Home Rulers, escape him. I took advantage of this to ask him for a few details on this organization. I learnt this: that the Orangeist army is by no means a fallacy, as one might imagine, and that it forms a sort of latent militia, with its active forces, and its reserve. At first, established as a kind of freemasonry, and formed in "circles" or "lodges," it comprises actually four divisions, subdivided into twenty-two brigades: each of these brigades consists of two or three regiments, infantry, cavalry, and artillery; in each regiment are sections and companies, each composed of affiliates belonging to the same district. Three divisions are recruited in Ulster proper; the fourth in Dublin and Cork, in Wicklow and in King's County. All those affiliates take the engagement to observe passive obedience and to render personal service on the first requisition of their supreme council; they furnish their own arms and recognise the authority of a commander-in-chief.

Does all this have any substantial existence besides what it has on paper? Do the Orangemen secretly drill, as it is averred, both for the infantry and the cavalry manœuvres? Is it true that most of the volunteer companies in Ulster are exclusively Orange companies? Lastly, are those volunteers really ready in case of an open rupture with Dublin, to take up their arms and fight for their cause? . . . Many people think it doubtful. The Home Rulers especially think it pure moonshine and humbug. I remember one of their papers publishing the following advertisement last year to show in what esteem they held the Ulster army:

Rotten Eggs! Rotten Eggs! Rotten Eggs!

Wanted: 100,000 rotten eggs, to be delivered in Tipperary, worthily to welcome 20,000 Orangemen, armed with rifles and guns, under command of the illustrious Johnson. Offers to be addressed to the printing office of this paper.

This certainly does not indicate a very exalted idea of the valour of the Orangeist forces on the part of the southern populations. But that does not mean that no other sugar plums shall be exchanged. In all civil wars such pleasantries take place, yet they do not prevent rivers of blood being shed. One fact alone is beyond doubt, that the Orange organization has immense ramifications among the regular troops, and is openly favoured by General Wolseley; that a large number of retired officers have entered it; that one would perhaps find it difficult to find one among the Queen's regiments ready to fire on the loyalists, and that the most ardent partisans of Home Rule hesitate to grant to the Irish Parliament the faculty of raising an armed force.

In conclusion, the last word in Ulster may very well be said by the Orangemen.

CHAPTER XVII.

LEX LICINIA.

It would have been pleasant to conclude these pages without recording too harsh a judgment against England, one of the two or three nations for ever dear to the thinker; one of those who possess a brain of her own, not merely a chain of nervous nodosities presiding over the organic functions; one of those who lead the Human Race along the hard road where it toilingly drags its miseries and delusions. It would have been pleasant at least to find some kind of extenuating circumstances for the attitude she maintains doggedly towards Ireland. But this is sheer impossibility.

All that can be pleaded on behalf of England is that she is truly unconscious of the wrong she has been doing for centuries, and that she firmly believes herself to have acted within her rights. Nations, still more than individuals, are the slaves of their temperament, of their faults and their qualities. Shall we call the tiger a murderer, or reproach vultures because they feed on human flesh? They obey their instincts, and merely follow the dictates of nature. So it is with nations. Considered no longer in the individuals that compose it, or in the intellectual *élite* that speaks in its name, but in the fifteen or twenty generations that have woven the woof of its annals, a people is an irresponsible and blind organism, fatefully obeying its impulses, be they noble or base.

Try to talk with a Protestant landlord about the wrongs and grievances of Ireland. He will tell you in all good faith that the Irish alone are to blame. Ignorant, slothful, given to drink, sly and cunning, a nation of liars,—weak, in a word, and vanquished beforehand,—this is the verdict he pronounces on them from the height of his respectable rent-roll. If they have failed in the struggle for life, it is because they came into it badly armed and unprepared. So much the worse for them,—let them make way for the stronger ones! Such is the theory.

There can be no doubt that it is put forward in all sincerity by a majority of Englishmen. But this does not prove that it rests on any sound foundation. It only proves once more that they are incapable of understanding anything about the Irish temperament.* This reasoning is merely the classic sophistry. They mistake the effect for the cause, and are blind to the fact that those vices they so bitterly reproach the Irish with, are the inevitable result of three centuries of bad administration and England's own work. Wherever it has been liberated from the English yoke, has not, on the contrary, the Irish race displayed abundant energy, activity, genius? Do not the Irish hold the first rank in the United States, in Canada, in Southern America, in Australia, wherever emigration has carried them. In England even are they not at the head of all liberal professions, letters, the daily press, the bar, science? Those who have seen and closely studied that nation, crushed under its secular burden, ground under the heel of the conqueror, cannot but feel surprised at the bare fact that it survives; and this fact alone presupposes the most admirable gifts. One could even question whether, deprived of the Irish Celt element, for leaven, for chiefs, for counsellors, in letters, and in assemblies, the heavy Anglo-Saxon race could ever have founded its flourishing colonies. These prosper, one may say, in direct proportion to the number of Irish that come to them, even as the mother island slowly decays

---

* See Appendix, p. 331.

in direct proportion to the number of her children that are driven from her shores.

Why should such slanderous explanations be sought for a fact sufficiently explained by history? The great misfortune of Ireland is not to be a nation less richly gifted than its conqueror, but only to be too small a nation, established in an open island. The Irish have been neither more vicious, nor more fanatical, nor more slothful than the English; they have been less numerous, less well armed; and John Bull, according to his deplorable custom, has taken advantage of their weakness for bullying them, for levying heavy toll on them, for bleeding them to death without mercy. He has taken their land, their freedom, their industry, and still wrests from them the product of their labour. And, to crown all, he dares to call them to account for their misery as for a crime—this misery, which is his own work, with all its wretched following of vices and degradation.

Before such a sight as this involuntary indignation must be felt. One wishes to say to the English—

"You pirates, begin first by giving back to Ireland all you have taken from her, and you shall see then if she be guilty of this poverty you consider as a crime! Let us reckon. Give her back her land, which your nobles occupy. Give her back the bravest of her sons, that you have driven to emigration. Give her back the habit of work which you have destroyed in her. Give her back the wealth which you prevented her accumulating, by forbidding her commerce and industry. Give her back the millions which you still exact every year upon the produce of her agricultural energy. Give her back the experience of freedom that you have so long crushed in her. Give her back the faculty of coolly reasoning about her beliefs, which persecution took from her. Give her back the right of self-government according to her genius, her manners, her will, that right which you declare sacred and imprescriptible for every nation, that you grant to your most insignificant colonies, to the meanest island of your Empire, and which you refuse to her, the biggest of all. Give her back all this, and let us see then if Ireland be all you say."

"Alas! from that national inheritance of which you robbed her one can only find now, recognise and therefore give back, the land and the money. The land stands always there; and money is not wanting in your coffers. A good impulse, then! All has to be paid for in this world—defeat and failure like anything else. If one lose a game, one must know how to pay for it gallantly. If one has, personally, or in the person of one's father, committed an unjust act, one must know how to atone for it. Your railway companies give indemnities to the families of those they have crushed to death. Yourselves, as a nation, have paid in the Alabama affair, once convinced of being in the wrong. Here also, in Ireland, the hour of Justice has come. Evidence is over. Your work rises in your throat and sickens you. You cannot any longer doubt, and your writers daily repeat it, that the cause of all Ireland's sufferings is in your spoliation, complicated by your administration. Well, the remedy is clear. Ireland herself points it out to you, and your conscience whispers it: you must give back her inheritance to Ireland, with the right of administering it according to her own lights."

England is fond of comparing herself to Rome, though it is Carthage rather that she resembles. She can find in Roman history a precedent for the solution that is obviously suited to Ireland. The *Lex Licinia*, promulgated in the year 376 before the Christian era, limited to 500 arpents, that is to say, almost exactly 500 acres, the extent of land that the patricians were entitled to possess in a conquered country. This was the law that the Gracchi wanted to bring to life again, and for which they paid the penalty of death. It has long been believed, and Mably repeated it with Montesquieu, that the question was the dividing of private property between all the citizens. Niebuhr and Savigny have re-established historical truth, and shown that the question at issue was merely the limitation of, or atonement for, usurpations that ruined the State by ruining the rural populations. It is a Licinian Law that is wanted in Ireland, and it is to be hoped that England will give it to her before long.

The disease of Ireland may be defined : the feudal system or landlordism, complicated by absenteeism and usury, having for its consequences extreme penury of capital, rural pauperism, and the incapacity for struggling against American competition.

The case of Ireland, more acute by reason of its special sphere, is only a striking instance of a fact that the legislators of the old world must necessarily take into account henceforth, the fact that the immense area of land newly cleared in the two Americas, in Australia, and India, are, four-fifths of them at least, the property of those that cultivate them personally. They have no other burden to bear than taxes, and are therefore in a condition of crushing superiority in the struggle with the countries in which dual ownership obtains. With an equal fruitfulness (and that of virgin soil is almost always greater), it is clear that the soil which supports only those that cultivate it, instead of two or three superposed classes of participants in its products, must always be able to give those products at a lesser cost price, and therefore will be able to throw them on the market at a lower rate. It is not merely common sense, it is the immutable course of human progress that condemns landlordism to disappear ere long from the face of the globe.

Reduced to its elementary terms, the Irish question stands thus : 12,000 landowners, of foreign origin, possessing almost the whole of the island ; 1940 of these proprietors detaining two-thirds of this soil ; 744 holding the half of it. All these lands parcelled out into insufficient holdings, and cultivated by 720,000 native farmers, for the most part entirely devoid of capital. The agricultural product of the island, divided between two schedules on the official rolls of the income tax : the first one of £2,691,788 only, representing the income of the 720,000 Irish farmers and their families ; the second, of £13,192,758, representing the income of the 12,000 English landlords. The half at least of this sum leaving the island every year, and being spent outside it by the *absentee* landlords. Not one farthing of this lordly income coming back to the soil, either directly or indirectly, in the shape of manure, buildings, or agricultural improvements ; nor to industry, which is nil. General pauperism, resulting from the feudal organization that stops development of wealth in its germ, and more and more unfits the country for a struggle with the more normally organized nations. Unpaid rents, landlords and tenants eaten up by usurers, a permanent conflict of interests shown at each term by three or four thousand evictions, without mentioning the still more numerous cases in which eviction is not carried out because it would prove useless. A universal bankruptcy ; a chronic state of social war ; a growing contempt of the law ; agrarian violence ; the suspension of public liberties ; a gradual return of the soil and its inhabitants to the savage condition ; a constant augmentation in the area of uncultivated land ; a regular emigration of the adult and able population ; a quarter of the remaining inhabitants living at the expense of the ratepayers, either on outdoor relief or in the workhouses; financial grievances, added to historical and political grievances; hunger sharpening the rancour of the vanquished race; its hatred of the conqueror shown periodically by the return to the House of Commons of 85 members whose only mandate is to obstruct the regular working of the British machinery. Such is the epitome of the results obtained in Ireland by the English after an occupation of seven centuries. Never did history register such a scandalous failure.

Vainly do Oxford and Cambridge, in order to explain or palliate it, resort to all their scholastic sophistry. Vainly it is endeavoured to discover its cause in some inherent vice of the Irish race, in their ignorance, their religion, their laziness, and even a sort of "melancholy" imparted to them, it is alleged, by the neighbourhood of the ocean (*sic*).

Ireland is not the only country edged by the Atlantic: neither is it the saddest. Her children are not in any marked degree more illiterate now-a-days than those of England, and if they were so for a long time—when they had to slip off to unlawful and clandestine "hedge schools" if they wanted to learn their alphabet—we know too well who was responsible for such an outrage on civilization. The Celts of Erin are Roman Catholics, it is true, but after all there are on our planet a certain number of nations who have not died yet of this religion. As for their political capacity, they vindicate it every day by the wisdom and firmness they display in sustaining the struggle against the oppressor.

One must bow to evidence and do justice to Ireland. And for this there are not two formulas. There is only one, in two articles :

1.—Expropriation of the landlords with a fair indemnity, to the profit of the Irish tenantry.

2.—The extension to Ireland of Home Rule, which is the invariable rule of all British possessions, near or far, guaranteed of course by all the precautions judged necessary for the security and unity of the United Kingdom.

It is the glory of Mr. Gladstone to have understood and to have had the moral courage to declare that there is no other solution. And as we think of this, is it not a strong argument in favour of the superior justice of agrarian revendications in Ireland, that it should have imposed itself to the reason of that illustrious politician, the most English assuredly of all the statesmen that have succeeded each other in office since the time of William Pitt ? Those common reasoners who rebel against a necessary restitution, should think of this. Here is an old man seventy-eight years of age, who, ever since he left Eton, had no other care, no other occupation than the affairs of his country; the most energetic, the most active and brilliant of leaders, the most experienced in finance; of all the orators in the British Parliament the most lucid and pungent; a refined scholar, an accomplished Hellenist, the possessor of an hereditary fortune that frees him from domestic cares, the son of a British merchant-prince, and the father of an Anglican clergyman, himself Protestant to the core, and fond of officiating in the place of his son in the church of Hawarden; a man whose predominant quality is his earnestness, and whose supreme rule of conduct is a well-regulated love of his country. This statesman, who has been ten times in office since the year, already so far from us, when he entered it under the leadership of Robert Peel, and who knows everything about the affairs of his country at home and abroad, has made his life-study of the Irish question. Twenty times in forty years has he attempted to grapple with it, to unravel it, to solve it. All the remedial measures that have been applied to the wounds of Ireland since 1860 had him for their initiator. He was the first to realize the odious wrong of an established Anglican

Church in that Catholic country. To him is due the political and intellectual enfranchisement of the Irish; it was he who gave them national schools and who put them (by dint of what Titanic struggles!) on the same electoral footing as the other British subjects. It was he who promoted, defended, and succeeded in passing all the Land Bills meant to soften the wretched fate of the Irish serf. Lastly, one must not forget it, he never hesitated, when he thought it necessary, to claim laws of repression against agrarian violence. Mr. Gladstone is assuredly no anarchist. He is neither a madman nor is he in his dotage. Never was his genius clearer, his word more eloquent. Add to this that this man, enamoured of power like all those who have passed their life in it, knew that he was courting a certain fall when he proposed his solution of the Irish question, and could entertain no doubt of the schism that would take place in his party on the subject. . . . .

And yet his conscience could oppose no resistance to the blinding light of facts. He clearly saw that palliatives were insufficient, and that there was an urgent need to take the evil at its root. As a conclusion to half a century spent in studying the case, and to twenty local attempts at healing it, after two or three thousand nights spent in the House of Commons in discussing the question under all its aspects, he comes forward to say: "*Justice to Ireland!* we must give back to her what was taken from her—her inheritance and her freedom!"

Can one suppose for a moment that Mr. Gladstone came to such a conclusion without the most decisive and powerful motives? Can anyone feel himself strong enough to hold opinions better founded than his on this matter? We must congratulate his adversaries on their happy self-confidence; but we cannot do so on their moral sense or on their modesty.

I.—Mr. Gladstone's Scheme.

Mr. Gladstone's scheme was framed in two organic Bills. By the first the British Government undertook to expropriate the landlords, and to redeem the Irish lands on a basis of twenty times the actual rent, to be paid in English Consols, at par. These lands would then be sold to the Irish tenants at a discount of 20 per cent., payable in forty-nine years by instalments equal to about half the former rent. The second Bill provided for the local government of Ireland, while it reserved for Great Britain the general control of the revenue and the right of keeping military forces in the island. Thanks to a coalition of a fraction of the Liberal party with the Tories, this programme fell to the ground at the General Election of 1886, and was set aside by Parliament.

It may be that the loss is not much to be regretted. Very likely Mr. Gladstone's scheme was, in his own thoughts, only meant as a trial, what we call a *ballon d'essai*. Excellent in its twofold principle, his solution had the very serious drawback of substituting, in the place of the 12,000 present landlords of Ireland—a single one, the State. It looked as if it solved all difficulties, and perhaps it would have caused fresh complications. In fact, it amounted to requiring that the unavoidable liquidation should be paid—by which people? By those who could least afford it—the Irish tenants. Whence might the poor devils have taken the money for their annuities? And even admitting that they could have found it, can one refuse to see that their culture, so wretched already, would have become still poorer? Has ever man chosen, to buy an estate, the moment when he is a confirmed bankrupt?

But it would have been to them a nett gain of one-half on their actual rent, it will be objected.

A nett gain of one-half *on nothing*, then, as they

Lex Licinia.

cannot afford to pay any rent just now, unless they deduct it from their capital (supposing that they have any), and there is no reason to suppose that things will be better for the next fifty years.

Besides, if you admit that by paying for forty-nine years half the actual rent as judicially fixed, the Irish tenants ought to have the ownership of the land, why, in the name of all that is fair, refuse to see that they have paid it more than ten times already, in the shape of excessive rent?

"They were free not to pay it and go out, with their goods and chattels," says my old friend, the Economist. I answer: No. They were not, for a thousand reasons, and had to obey the will of the vampires, as long as it was strictly possible.

Either the tenants, having become proprietors in name but not in reality (or, as it were, proprietors of a shadow of land mortgaged for half a century), would have paid their annuity,—and in that case they were as poor as before; or they would not have paid it, and then the Liberal party would have heard a fine din!

In fact the Gladstone plan rested on an entirely chimerical hope: that of settling the Irish question without its costing a penny to the British Exchequer. To entertain such a hope is clearly to prove that one sees indeed the evil, but without descrying its deeper cause.

This cause lies in the IMPOSSIBILITY to the modern tenants, in the face of the competition of better organized countries, and generally under the present conditions of the world's agriculture, TO PAY ANY RENT WHATEVER.

The Irish tenant is a bankrupt, because he has paid, for too long a time already, the rent that he could not afford. The land is impoverished for the very same reason. Now, to sell it to a penniless buyer is absurd enough; but to pretend to believe that the penniless buyer shall render it prosperous and make it yield riches, is perhaps more absurd still.

Such illusions ought to be discarded. If England really wants to settle the Irish question, as her honour and her true interest both command her to do, she must manfully accept the idea of a pecuniary sacrifice and a real restitution. It would be useless to cheat herself into acceptance of half-measures. She had much better weigh the real cost of an imperious duty, pay it, and square matters once for all.

Not only must she give, *gratuitously give away* as a present, the land to the Irish tenant, but she must provide him, at the lowest rate of interest, with the capital necessary for putting that land in working order.

This consummation might perhaps be attained at a lesser cost than would at first sight appear possible,—let us name a figure,—at a cost of one milliard francs, or £40,000,000. But this milliard should be forthcoming in cash, presented by the British nation to the sister isle as a free gift, a premium paid for peace, or rather a lump sum of conscience-money, such as we see sometimes advertised in the columns of the *Times*.

II.—AN OUTSIDER'S SUGGESTION.

The ideal solution for the innumerable difficulties of the Irish question would evidently be the *tabula rasa*,—the hypothesis that would transform Ireland into a newly-discovered island of virgin soil, barren and uninhabited, where England had just planted her flag, and out of which she wished to get the fullest value in the shortest possible time.

What would her policy be in such a case? She would begin by surveying the whole extent of her new acquisition, by parcelling it out in lots carefully, then by calling in colonists and capital.

To the immigrants that came without any other wealth than their stalwart arms, she would make gratuitous concessions of small lots of land, accompanied by seeds, agricultural implements, and an exemption from taxes during a limited period of time. To those who came with capital, she would give more important plots of ground, either demanding a premium of occupation more or less high, shortening the period of exemption for taxes, or again elevating the rate of those taxes. Most likely, too, she would favour the establishment of an Agricultural Bank that would advance to the new colonists such moneys as they desired, according to their wants, their chances of success, and the individual securities they presented.

In reality it cannot be supposed that in Ireland the past, the vested interests and the settled habits of centuries, can be erased. But at least one can try to come near to this ideal; and besides, this island presents, over the barren and uncultivated one, the advantage of having a ready-made population; the country, its climate, its soil, are known; there is a large proportion of able workmen, valuable house property, no inconsiderable provision in agricultural implements, not to mention several thousand head of horse, oxen, sheep, and pigs ready imported.

The advantages of this over a virgin island are, therefore, very clear; they are visibly stronger than the drawbacks, and success is certain if measures of the kind we allude to are vigorously carried out.

England, then, must begin by buying out, not only the properties of the landlords, but also, and this is only justice, the interest that a large number of farmers possess in those lands under the name of tenant-right. The area of cultivated land in Ireland (exclusive of towns) is, in round numbers, fifteen million acres. Before all, the basis of indemnity granted to the landlords must be fixed.

Mr. Gladstone proposed the basis of twenty times the actual rent, as judicially fixed. This seems an exorbitant price, for various reasons. The first reason is that no leased land under the sun normally yields to its owner, at present, anything like the interest supposed by such a valuation. The second reason is that the landlords' property in Ireland has actually no real value whatever; it could not find a purchaser, probably, at the price of three times the nominal rent, were it put up for sale (let anyone who commands capital, and who looks for a secure investment, consider whether he would ever dream of buying Irish land, just now, at any price). The third reason is that the true responsibility of the Irish disease rests with those very landlords who never did their duty by the country. Granted that their faults (one would rather say crimes) ought to be covered by the benefit of prescription, and that a fair indemnity ought to be given them or their creditors if they are dispossessed by measures of public sanitation, it would look ridiculous,—indecent to go to the length of rewarding them for their moral and economical failure by a disproportionate indemnity taken out of the pocket of the British taxpayer.

When one hears, therefore, Mr. Gladstone speak of giving the landlords twenty times the nominal rent of their land, one is reduced to admit that his idea was to bribe them into acquiescence to his scheme by an exorbitant premium. The Irish landlords did not understand their true interest; they did not see that they should have thrown into the scale the weight of their votes. Very likely they were wrong. They may say good-bye to the Gladstone indemnity; they will never see it again. For the longer they wait to settle this question, the more must farm-rent dwindle away and indemnity shrink to nothingness.

It seems that, at present, in fixing it on the basis of twelve times the judicial rent, the British nation would show great liberality. It would be equivalent to saying that Irish land, as an investment, is worth one-third the capital in English Consols that bears the same interest, which is certainly paying it an unexpected compliment.

As for the tenant-right of the farmer, which it is

equally indispensable to redeem if all is to be cleared and there are to be no more conflicts of interests, let us admit that it is worth, on the whole, three or four times the judicial rent. Very likely again this is excessive. But this matters little practically, as will be shown further on. We find thus, for the aggregate interest vested in the Irish soil and subject to indemnity, a common rate of sixteen times the judicial rent.

The average of this judicial rent is ten shillings per acre. For fifteen millions of cultivated acres to be redeemed, this would therefore give a total sum of 120 millions sterling to be paid. Thanks to this indemnity of expropriation, the English nation would become absolutely free to dispose of these lands as she pleased.

But where are those 120 million pounds to be found? and they must be found over and above the capital necessary for the working of these lands, since we admitted in principle that it would be necessary to find it in most cases. This is the way:

As a first outlay, we have admitted that the British Exchequer would put down £40,000,000 sterling in the shape of Consols at par. That capital represents an interest of about one million sterling and a quarter, or an annual tax of about ninepence per head. This certainly would not be a high price to pay for such a precious advantage as the suppression of the Irish plague. There is no decade in which a great nation does not pay more for some unlucky and useless venture—the Afghanistan campaign, as a case in point.

To these 40 millions sterling, sacrificed by the wealthiest of European nations to its internal peace, shall be added the resources proper to Ireland. These are no despicable ones. Ireland, taxed much lower than Great Britain, nevertheless contributes no less than eight millions sterling, in round numbers, to the general revenue of the United Kingdom.

Of these £8,000,000 about £4,286,519 go to the keeping of the army of occupation and the administration of finances; in other words, to the services meant to remain "imperial" in the hypothesis of Home Rule. About £3,744,462 are paid for the services that would, in this hypothesis, come into the province of the Irish Parliament, viz., public works, law courts, tax-gathering, local administration, registrations, land-surveying, lunatic asylums, schools, prisons, and the like. It seems that a new and poor country, as we suppose Ireland to turn out, ought not to pay for such services as liberally as does wealthy England, and that a reduction of a third on these heads, or £1,250,000, is perfectly feasible. That is about the income for £40,000,000 in English Consols. Here, then, we have sufficient provision for a second milliard in the shape of *interest*.

The interest for the third milliard would easily be raised in the shape of additional taxes, if Irish agriculture were freed from any other charges. That would only increase the annual taxation by about a sixth part, and would not even then put it on a level with the incidence of English taxation. Ireland, on her side, might well do this slight sacrifice to the cause of social and political peace.

There, then, we have the £120,000,000 wanted (in the shape of a special loan, emitted and guaranteed by England), which are found—a third by each of the high contracting parties; a third by a reduction of 33 per cent. on all services that would have become purely Irish.

How ought this magnificent lump of money to be used to make it bear all it can? By lodging the whole in the coffers of a special *Bank of Liquidation*, that would be entrusted with all the operation. This bank, strong in her guaranteed capital of £120,000,000, invested, if necessary, with the power of emitting special paper-money, begins by paying all the lands on the basis fixed upon by law. This implies only, at the most, an outlay of £90,000,000. These lands the bank divides into three classes.

Class A.—The fee simple of the first class, composed of the holdings under £10 a year, is simply transferred to their actual holders (as would be done in an infant colony in order to attract inhabitants), subject to the single proviso that these lands shall be cultivated after a given system, and according to certain rules, and taken back by the public domain, if this condition be not observed.

Let us remark, in passing, that this free gift will, in the majority of cases, be only the legalization of a *de facto* gratuitous occupation, most of these small tenants having, for the last three or four years, stopped paying any rent to the landlords.

Where, in that case, will be their advantage? it might be asked. They will be no richer for having become landowners in point of law, as they are now in fact.

This is a material error, as shown by the example of our peasant proprietors in France. One of the chief reasons that prevent the small Irish tenant endeavouring to get all he can out of his land is precisely the rooted wish in his mind not to work for the benefit of the landlord. From the day that he shall be certain of keeping the entire fruit of his labour to himself, he will emulate the French Celt; he will submit himself to the hardest privations and the most unremitting toil; he will abundantly manure his land, ceaselessly tend it, turn it again and again; he will make it yield all it can. Anyhow, if he does not, he will have only himself to blame for it.

Class B.—The second class of land, composed of holdings from 15 to 20 acres and over, is sold to its actual holders for the price of their tenant right, if they be willing to accept this privilege. In the contrary case, the tenant right is paid down to them at the rate fixed upon by experts, and the fee simple is put up for sale by auction. The ultimate proprietors of these domains of average extent receive, by the hands of the local agents for the *Bank of Liquidation*, every facility to form themselves into unions for the collective culture of their land. They remain, however, free to cultivate it themselves and in their own fashion.

Class C.—The third portion of the soil, formed by the choicest land, shall be put aside in each district to form a great domain where experiments shall be tried and examples given in agriculture—a domain managed by official agronomists, and cultivated by associations of agricultural labourers, salaried partly in kind on the product of the land, partly by participation in the nett profits. Not only shall there be introduced on those great domains, together with the finest breeds of cattle, the most perfect and scientific modes of culture, but, besides, public demonstrations and lectures shall be made, agricultural pupils shall be formed, and seeds of first quality shall be given at cost price. These model-farms alone remain the property of the State, and are inalienable.

Thus would be constituted at once, together with a class of peasant proprietors, the middle and great cultures which are equally wanting in Ireland.

Special laws abolish entail in the island, submit to expropriation (for 25 years at least) any owner non-resident on his property, and forbid, under pain of heavy fines, to hold or give on lease any parcel of land under 12 acres.

Other laws, imitated from the *Homestead Exemption* of the United State, protect the peasant against debt. The *Liquidation Bank*, after having set the new system in motion, secures its working by advancing at the lowest rate of interest the capital wanted by the small and middling landowners, which must before long kill usury and drive it from the country. This bank is, in every sense, the organ and focus of a fiduciary circulation that is amply sufficient, on this broad basis, for all the financial wants of agricultural industry.

Thus, the whole revenue of the land remaining in the country, circulating freely, and incessantly undergoing its normal transformations, health returns by degrees to the social body. There is no longer any question of "unemployed" labourers; on the contrary, it is rather hands that are wanted on all those flourishing estates which have day-work to offer, not only to the owners of small holdings, but even to the unemployed of Great Britain.

And so England begins rapidly, though indirectly, to recover her advance, owing to the quick increase in the returns of the Income Tax; in perhaps four or five years, that increase covers the interest of her £40,000,000. It comes to say that her real outlay turns out to be only a tenth or a twelfth part of that advance. Emigration suddenly receives a check. Nay, a new, liberated, prosperous Ireland sees her children flock back to her shores from abroad, enriched and reconciled, bringing home their capital with their experience. For the Irishman ever keeps in his heart unimpaired the love of his mother country, and will return to her as soon as he can.

Let us carry our hypothesis further.

At the same time when she gave up the responsibilities of the local government of Ireland, England has transmitted them to the representatives of the Irish nation.

Are those representatives to form immediately a single Parliament sitting at Dublin, or are they for the present to be divided into four provincial assemblies for Leinster, Munster, Connaught, and Ulster? This question is of small importance, at least at the beginning. Let the first step be taken; an united Ireland will only be a matter of time. The best way in such cases is to follow the expressed wish of the populations; and supposing that Ulster, or at least a part of Ulster, vote for the continuation of the present *régime*, why should not those territories be excepted from the new arrangements, and either be left *in statu quo* or joined politically to Scotland, of which they are a geological as well as an ethnical dependency? But I cannot help thinking that if the above system was submitted to the Antrim tenants themselves, they would not be backward to see its advantages.

On the whole question the last word should remain to the voter. If a majority of the electors of Scottish Ireland spoke in favour of Home Rule, what could be objected to them? That they will eventually be oppressed by the Catholics? No great fear of that, I should think; and besides, efficient measures could be taken, guarantees found against that danger; but no such caution will be really wanted. The influence of the Catholic clergy in Ireland has for its principal basis the political state of the country. The day when difficulties are cleared up, national education will soon have put an end to the reign of clericalism in Ireland as elsewhere.

One cannot help feeling firmly convinced that Mr. Gladstone's formula, "Home Rule and Abolition of Landlordism," taken in its most general meaning, and applied with a spirit both prudent and liberal, will suffice to heal in a few years the disease of Ireland. Public wealth will rise by degrees, feelings of hatred will die away, the rapidity of the cure will take the world by surprise. Has not already the adoption of the Irish programme by a large number of Englishmen belonging to the Liberal party been sufficient to bring about a partial reconciliation between the two countries? We have seen Irish orators come and preach the Liberal gospel in England, and reciprocally, English orators go and bring the word of peace to Ireland. That alone is an augury of success, a symptom of healing and pacification.

Will it be objected that this is a Utopian picture, an unpractical scheme, or simply one of difficult execution? As for me, the more I look into the matter, the more settled grows my belief that three things only are requisite for substituting so much good for so much evil, viz., money, steadiness of purpose and conscience. Nobody will say that the English have ever shown a lack of steadiness in the pursuit of success; money they have in abundance; will they be wanting in conscience? This is scarcely to be feared. Conscientiousness of a more or less enlightened kind is a characteristic of the Englishman, and it is his highest praise. Men are constantly to be met in England who rule their conduct on the principles of an inward law. It is true that, by a natural consequence, many are good only in name, and their display of conscience is only a sham; but as our great moralist has said, "Hypocrisy is a homage which vice renders to virtue," and wherever vice is obliged to wear a mask, virtue is bound to conquer.

A great transformation, the instruments of which are the press, the steam-engine, and the telegraph, has been slowly developing throughout the world during the last few years: a new and powerful influence has been born that might be named "obligatory justice through publicity." Tennyson has spoken of "the fierce light that beats upon a throne;" thrones now-a-days scarcely exist except in name; the will of the people has taken their place. But let Governments call themselves republics or monarchies, they are equally submitted to that pitiless ray of light which is the ever-wakeful eye of the press, the uncompromising publicity which ignores either rank or station. How many examples of it have we not seen at home! To quote a recent one, take that wretched Schnæbelé affair. Only fifteen years ago there would have been found in it reasons ten times sufficient to bring about a war for those who wanted it. Not so in our days. In less than twenty-four hours the press had brought to light the most minute details of the affair, exposed the naked truth to the eyes of the world, photographed the place where the incident had occurred, submitted, in short, to the great public judge all the evidence of the case. One had to tender apologies under pain of being called the aggressor, and the whole affair evaporated into smoke.

Such results are perhaps the clearest gain that modern progress has given us. If our age has a superiority over the preceding ages, it is assuredly to have succeeded in making injustice more difficult to practise. More and more henceforward will great national crimes become impossible. Mr. Gladstone's chief merit will be to have understood it before anybody in England, and to have been emphatically the man of his time. In spite of friends and adversaries he has dared to utter the truth, and say: "We must give back to Ireland what we have taken from her. The good of England imperiously demands that sacrifice, for we are entering an age when the honour of a great nation should not even be suspected."

He is actually the only statesman in Europe who follows a policy of principle; the only one seeking the triumph of his opinions by the sole help of reason. All the others, from the most famous to the most obscure or passing politician, are only jobbers. Disraeli had too much of the mountebank about him to have been able to secure the respect of posterity. Gortschakoff was only a courtier of the old school; Cavour a clever lawyer; Thiers a dwarf, in a moral and political, as in a physical, sense. Bismarck profits by a state of affairs which he did little or nothing to create, and at the most is the belated representative in our times of fossil feudalism. Gladstone alone is a truly modern statesman, and therefore is destined to be set by history above all his contemporaries, if only he succeeds in carrying out his great enterprise; for the more we go the more nations shall be restricted to politics of principle, both because all other systems are exploded, and because the diffusion of learning will be for the future an almost insuperable obstacle to petty or brutal diplomatic conspiracies.

Great Britain, it is earnestly to be hoped, will consent to follow her great leader in the way he has shown to her. She is offered the most splendid opportunity of doing what no nation has achieved as yet,—atoning, of her own free will, for centuries of injustice, and trying one of the noblest social experiments that can ever be attempted. It would be the beginning of a new era in the history of human societies, and pure glory for those who initiated it. Not only could such results be attained at little cost, but the most obvious, the most pressing interest of England invites her to the enterprise. Let her make haste. After having affirmed for half a century the sovereignty of peoples, and their right to govern themselves according to their will, she cannot give herself the lie at home. After having protested against Bomba and the Bulgarian atrocities, she cannot in her own dominions remain beneath "the unspeakable Turk." After having assumed before the world the attitude of a systematic foe to slave-trade and all kinds of oppression or cruelty, after having carried it even to maudlin sensitiveness, as in the case of pigeon-shooting, "birds' corpses on women's hats," and the like, she cannot decently carry on the slow destruction of a sister race through starvation. She cannot and she will not do it, for it would be branding herself for ever as Queen of Humbug, Empress of Sham.

APPENDIX.

EXTRACTS FROM SOME LETTERS ADDRESSED WITHIN THE LAST TWO YEARS TO AN IRISH LANDLORD BY HIS TENANTS.

The *Times* has published, on October 10, 1887, an exceedingly interesting batch of letters selected from some three hundred addressed within the last two years to an Irish landowner by his tenants. As the editor of those letters wrote most appropriately, there is perhaps no means whereby truer insight can be obtained into the ways and habits of the Irish peasantry than by studying the letters written by the people themselves. Typically enough, however, the same editor only saw in those letters how "unbusiness-like and illogical is the Irish tenant," and "the various reasons that an Irishman gives for not paying his rent. One is unable to pay because his uncle is confined to bed, and his daughter suffering from a sore eye; another because a relative has died; a third because his brother-in-law has brought an action against him for money lent, and he has had to pay; one because his family is small, and another because it is large; another—and this is the most common excuse—because he has been unable to sell his stock; another because his wife has a sore hand; another because of the death of a cow; another because the weather is severe and there is a sheriff's bailiff obstructing him from making up the rent; another because it was God's will to take all the means he had; another because of the agitation."

Reasons which, it may be seen, appear to the English eye entirely ridiculous and unbusinesslike.

What strikes a Frenchman most, on the other hand, in the letters, is their touching simplicity, the appalling instability of a budget that the least domestic mishap is enough to upset, and the fruitless attempt of the poor man to penetrate into the real cause of the burden under which he is panting; in the comments, the utter incapacity of the British landlord to understand his Irish tenantry even when he is a good landlord, which is obviously (perhaps too obviously) the case here.

The letters are thus characteristic in more than one sense. Whatever the angle under which they are read, they undoubtedly remain first-class documentary evidence.

To * * * * , Esq.   *8th Jany.*, 1887.

Sir,—I received a letter yesterday from Mr. G—— who demanded the payment of £31 0s. 6d., rent due up to 29 Sept. 1886. I was in with Mr. G—— this day & he told me that he had no further instructions than what was contained in his note. Now my Uncle has been confined through illness to his bed since last June, & my daughter has been under medical treatment since last September for a sore eye which proceeded from a bad tooth, & I even had to pay the Dentist ten shillings for extracting it, as the Doctor could not do so. I trust you will kindly take into consideration my position and stay proceedings, & I will send you £18 next Saturday & the remainder about the 13th February, the day after fair of K——.

Your obedt. Servant
* * * *

The following is also from the same man :—

Sir,—I would have sent you the remainder of the rent on the day mentioned but the old man died & I had extra expenses but if you would kindly wait until about the 25th of March I will be able to let you have it.

Your obedient servant
* * * *

9th March, 1887.

Sir,—I have yours of the 4th inst. & am very sorry to say I have met a reverse & cant pay up to my word. I took a Brother-in-law to live with me—he was a tenant of your property who lost the power of his limbs & obliged to get into Hospital. his daughter my niece who I reared went to America she died there after saving a good deal of money her father after much trouble got £200 of it & after being 17 years in the Hospital he had to leave it having means to live & he requested to come to live with me which I allowed, & being maintained as one of my family for 12 months up to Wedy. last he now sued me for £50 which he lent me while here. He is at other lodgings & subject to evil advice but he fell out with me while here & since has been most ungrateful. I done my best to get this law put back but failed & had to pay the money I had made to pay my rent. I am much grieved being obliged to ask to the middle of next month to pay it. I wont have any fairs sooner to sell my stores but I will surly have it about the 20th April if not sooner. You may be sure only what happened me I would have paid up to my promise.

      Your obt servt

       * * * *

10th March.

MR. ———. After all I built & what I ow in shops & from the loss of sheep I am not abell to pay but if you forgive me this half year's rent you will save me from destruction, and if so I will keep it a profound sacred. I promis I will never again ask anything of you & will be punctual in future. my family is small & my health not good to go travell. I brought a dale of money in to this farm 5 years ago and it is all gon now. I apeal to your kind & genariss hart to do this for me & may the almitey god give your self & your children the Kingdom of hevan.

    I remain most respectfully

       * * * *

January 9*th.*

DEAR SIR,—In reply to youre noat I am verrey sorrey that I can do nothing at the presant it is out of my power I have nothing to sell unlss I sell what I have to ate my self and seven littel children. I had but one calf to sell to pay you and it was the will of provedence to take him, he died. I have but one cow & I had hur in the fair of N—— and all I could get for her was four pounds, so if you presede with the law as yore lawyer sayes he will I must sell hur to pay you

Your humbel tennant

* * * *

August 31.

SIR,—I promised the rent after the fair of K—— in June. I had three calves in it & covld not sell. I took three months grass for them to see could I do better. I intend to have them in D—— on the 12th & if I sell them I will send the rent after that. I would have wrote only expecting to have the rent before this. My wife took a sore hand & is in hospital this two months & is in it still so its poor times with me.

Your tennant

* * * *

11*th March.*

SIR,—In reply to your letter dated 5th inst. I beg to ask your honour the favour of a few days grace. I hope to be able to meet your demands by the time you call to collect your rents in April. In the meantime I might have an opportunity of setting the fields in Con acre.

Being a lone widow with two helpless children one of them of weak intellect I hope your honour will kindly consider my case.

I am Sir your Honour's most obedient & humble servant

* * * *

January 19.

SIR,—I received your letter. it is not in my power to make money for you now as I had to borrow some of your last rent which is not all paid yeat on account of the death of my fine cow that died. I will use my best endavours against May.

Your ob. servt

* * * *

September 26.

DEAR SIR,—I make apail to you at the present time that I am endeavring at this time to make up the rent. Now I would have it sooner but the weather for the harvest was savere, sore I could not help it Der Sir, there is a man who is a Sheirf's baliff is going to injure me & to obstruct me in making up the rent for you which I would hope soon to have value for. Dear Sir I apail to you that you will not allow but Dis allow injuring a poor tenant who is endeavring to make up the rent. I would say one thing that I believe he is at least without maners. I apail to you that you will not allow to obstruct making out rent as quck as posible. one thing I wonder much that you would permit him or such as him any place. I will refrain on that presnt. I will ask this request off Mr. —— as soon as I can get the rent will he be kind enough to take it from me. I will ask the favour of you to give return as it may plaise you. Excuse my hand riting.

Yours truly

* * * *

August 2nd.

Mr. ——— I received Mr. G——'s letter on the 31st of July. I am sorry I am not able to pay at preasant. I am willing to pay my rent but it was God's will to take all the mains I had intended to meet you. I hope you will be so kind to give time untell October, as it is so hard to make money

Your obt. servent

Pat. F——.

Wensdy 19th.

* * * * Esq. Sir,—I received your letter & will send you the rent as soon as I can. There was no price for cattle in the fairs that ispast, in fact the could not be sold atol. I expect to make the rent in the fair of K———. I could always pay my rent but this cursed agetation has destroyed our country but I hope the worst of it is over

I remain Your Obedient Servant

* * * *

The following letters also relate to the payment of rent :—

October 10.

Sir,—I did not receive your letter ontill this Day. It has given me a great surprise   I hope your Honour will not put me to cost   I have a little best to sell, and after the fair in C——, a thursday I will send it to yo and I hop yo will not put me to cost.   I hop your honour will feel for me

truly

* * * *

October 4th.

Mr. ——   Sir,—I was again disappointed in the fair at N—— in selling my cattle and I must ask time of you till I get sale for if possible I will sell them in the fair of C——   do not once imagine that I am not enclined to pay but I never was offered a price for my cattle.   I was speaking to some of the tenants and the would wish to see you in N—— the rent day as the want to know what you want for your land

Yours respectfully,

* * * *

Sir,—I was very sory to see your hon goeing back without the rient.

I was willing to pay that day but I could not.   I send you my half-year's rent £13 10, so I hope your hon will luck after turf for me there is no ous in asking it of Mr. F—— There is to banks idle on the tients part on F——— and Mrs. N——— has 30 banks set this year so I count it very unfare if we doent get one The old men was geoing to kill us when we did not pay your hon the day you ware in N——— We ware all sory we did not settle that day

    I remane your obdient servant

              * * * *

rember the tturf.

The following is in the same handwriting as the last, but signed by another tenant:—

DEAR SIR,—You spoke of referring to Mr. F——— for turf, we did not like to intrupeed (query, interrupt) yur hon at that time. Well sir there is too banks of your own on the tients part an Mrs. N——— is giveing turf to men on the five different estates Every one that wonted turf got it but two tients no one els wonts it besids, so I hope your hon will luck to us. I am willing to pay my way if I get a chance. N——— D——— has turf this 40 years No one wants it but P——— F——— & M——— T———. We would pay your hon ondly for the rest

    Believe me Your obedient servent

            M——— T———.

do what your hon can about the turf

November 23*rd* 86.

HONOURED SIR,—I got both your letters & replidd to the first & directed it to D——— in which I asked for a little time to pay the rent I had some young cattle in the fair of K———

and did not sell them. It will greatly oblige me if your Honour will give me time untill the Christmas fair of F—— as I have some pigs to sell that will meet this rent & that would leave me the cattle to meet the May rent as the young cattle I have is not fit to sell at preasant.

I feel sorry to have to trespass on your Honour, but the times are bad and it is hard to make money, but I hope we will soon have better times under the present Government, and that all those mob laws will soon be at an end.

I remain your humble servant,
* * * *

It shows a curious state of things when a would-be tenant thinks it necessary to assure the landlord that he knows the farm belongs to him:—

April 12, 1887.

To Mr. * * * *

SIR,—Just a few lines to let your honour know that my father is very delicate for the past tow months and not expected to recover. I would like to let your honour know that it was mee that minded your Property for the last ten years. I know that this place always belongs to you and that the emprovements cost no one But your self a shilling. I would like to know how mutch my father is in your dept.

I remain your honors faiteful servant,
JAMES T——.

Appendix.

The following contain offers of cattle in lieu of rent, a form of payment which Irish tenants are always anxious to adopt if they can, for though they declare there will be no difference about the price, they always expect the landlord to give them considerably more than the market value :—

January 18.

DEAR SIR,—I am not able to answer you with money at present. I have the heifer that I told you of and if you wish I will send her to T—— for you, and I expect your honor and I wont differ.

Your obedient servent,

PATRICK F——Y.

Jany 5*th.*

SIR,—I have 5 nice bullocks to sell if you would buy them. I have no other way of paying the rent.

F—— D——.

October 14*th.*

DEAR SIR and pleas your honour,—I hope in you that you wont buy all the cattle you want in S—— town. Patrick D—— has a lot greasing with the father-in-law at C——; he intends to meet your honour with them. Pleas, Sir, leave room for three Bullocks, I have them greasing with you above the road all the summer.

Your faithful servant,

MICHL. T——.

I am setten some of my children and it has left me bare in monney.

Novr 12*th*.

DEAR SIR,—I will give three two-year-old Bullicks good owns for next May rent. I will leave the vallue to your honour when you come down before Christamas. I was offered £15 pounds for the three last June ; £5 each from Mr. ——— the Miller of C———. I never took them out since. I have no father for them. Your honour has plenty of straw to give them, the will make good Bullocks on it. Your honour must get them les than vallue

Your truly faithfull servent,

* * * *

THE END.

INDEX OF SELECTED PLACE NAMES

INDEX OF SELECTED PLACE NAMES

Antrim, Co.   47, 275–86, 290, 324
Armagh, Co.   85, 290
Aughrim   236
Australia, emigration to   2, 37
Ballinillane   123
Belfast   273, 287–95
Blackrock   20
Boyne, river   88
Bray   20
Bushmills   277, 279
Caherciveen   123, 147, 155
Carlingford   71
Carrick-a-Rede   286
Castleisland   119
Castlemaine   137
Cavan, Co.   85
Clare, Co.   130, 197, 215, 217
Cobh [Queenstown]   190–92
Coleraine   275
Colyherbeer   116
Connaught   32, 52, 84, 86, 324
Connemara   47, 52
Cork   133, 190
Cork, Co.   140
Corrib, Lough   236
Derg, Lough   237, 250
Derry   274–5
Derry, Co.   63, 85, 290
Dingle   147
Donegal, Co.   63, 85, 230, 275
Donegal Bay   52
Down, Co.   290
Drogheda   86, 273
Dublin   7–25, 26, 63, 208, 209; Castle   14–16, 55; Liberties   38–45, 57; Phoenix Park   14; Trinity College   22–8
Dublin Bay   6, 20
Dundalk   273
Dundalk Bay   52
Dun Laoghaire [Kingstown]   5, 6, 20
Dunluce Castle   278, 279, 286
Dunseverick   286
Ennis   197, 198
Enniskillen   271
Faha   123
Fermanagh, Co.   85
Foynes   50, 215
Freemount   123
Galway   60, 86, 234, 236

Garavogue, river 256
Giant's Causeway 47, 276, 278, 280–86
Gill, Lough 256
Glenbeigh 151
Grianán of Aileach 63
Gwingullier 115
Holyhead, Wales 5
Innisfallen 66, 97, 99
Irishtown 204
Kells (Co. Kerry) 123
Kenmare 97–9, 102, 105, 116
Kenmare, river 147
Kerry, Co. 47, 52, 58, 96, 109–56
Kilfree Junction 269
Killarney 63, 96–108
Kilrush 215
Leinster 52, 324
Liffey, river 7, 29
Limerick 88, 215, 219, 222–4
Listowel 128, 133–5
Mayo, Co. 58
Milltown (Co. Kerry) 124
Molahiffe 116
Muckross 97–9, 104
Munster 52, 84, 324
Pleaskin 286
Portnoffen Bay 286
Portrush 276–7, 286

Raphoe [Raphre] 63
Rathmore 123
Ross Island 99
Shannon, river 46, 50, 86, 215–17
Shinnagh 115
Skelligs 155
Sligo 256
Strangford 71
Tarbert 216
Timoleague 174–5
Tralee 116, 121
Trughanarkny 116
Tyrone, Co. 85
Ulster 32, 51, 52, 85, 91, 271–95, 324
United States of America 2, 51, 67, 91, 188–9, 204
Valentia Island 51, 155
Waterford 74
Westport 206
Wexford 71, 86, 233
Wicklow, Co. 20, 47
Woodford 236–55, 261